A Different Kind of Vow

A Different Kind of Vow

Rewriting My Happily Ever After

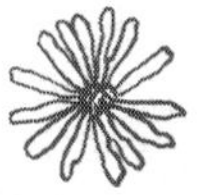

LAURIE COLLISTER

SHE WRITES PRESS

Published in 2026 by
She Writes Press, an imprint of The Stable Book Group

32 Court Street, Suite 2109
Brooklyn, NY 11201
https://shewritespress.com
Library of Congress Control Number: 2026900509
ISBN: 979-8-89636-112-1
eISBN: 979-8-89636-113-8

Interior Designer: Tabitha Lahr

Printed in the United States

Names and identifying characteristics have been changed to protect the privacy of certain individuals.

AUTHOR'S NOTE

This memoir is based on the author's diary entries and personal recollections. Events, conversations, and settings have been recreated to the best of the author's memory. Certain names, identifying details, and locations have been altered to protect privacy, and the chronology of events may have been compressed for readability. The statements, opinions, and interpretations herein are solely those of the author and are not intended to defame, disparage, or cause harm to any person, organization, religion, ethnic group, or gender identification.

To all who wish to rewrite their happily ever after

Life can only be understood backwards,
but it must be lived forwards.
—Søren Kierkegaard

CONTENTS

PROLOGUE

"Get out! Get out now!" a woman screamed, as she pounded on my door.

I flung the door open to find Sherry, the high school principal who lived next door.

"My condo's on fire!" she cried, yanking my arm.

We ran to the street as sirens echoed in the distance.

At the curb, we waved our arms wildly over our heads to flag down two fire engines careening down the street.

Out of breath, Sherry explained to the captain that her french fries had caught fire.

Firemen toting hoses raced past us. But the two-story fire proved too much. Sherry's condo burned to the ground, and mine came close.

As I stretched out in bed at a nearby Comfort Inn, I thought about the calamity that had cut a steady path through my recent past. I'd broken up with my fiancé. I'd totaled my car. And my home had almost burned down.

While most people would be reeling from such loss, I remained eerily calm, even relieved. God had lit a match. All that destruction was actually a blessing. It had cleared away all that no longer worked in my life.

The next day, I ventured back home to assess the damage. The disaster crew in fluorescent yellow vests were already hard at work. They'd piled the kitchen cabinets—now charred wood—in my interior patio. They'd ripped up my carpet, exposing the cement subfloor. And the few clothes that had not burned had been packed off to an ozone chamber in Burbank. "You know, to get rid of the smoke," a worker explained.

I poked my head in my second-floor office, afraid of what I'd find. Amazingly, my diaries still lined the floor-to-ceiling shelves. My most cherished possessions had been spared. The three hundred diaries spanned a critical period of my life: from 1986, when I'd first moved to LA at the age of thirty-three, to the present, January 2003, just as I'd hit the half-century mark.

I asked the disaster crew to transfer the volumes to the trunk of my car. Perhaps God had saved them for a reason. I vowed to read each one before another catastrophe *did* destroy them. And so, I launched a new pastime. Every night after work, I'd devour another volume.

My journal entries felt like pieces of a jigsaw puzzle. Each irregular shape defined a fragment of my life—a swatch of green grass or an inch of blue sky. But the thousands of pieces needed to be fit together. Only then could I see the complete picture of my life trajectory: the expanse of blue sky and the vast vista of rolling lawn.

I love clues. I love confidences. I love the clandestine. In fact, I'd devoted much of my professional life to unraveling secrets, first as a litigation paralegal, then as a market analyst, and finally as a writer and business journalist. The trouble was I'd never cracked the code of my own life. Maybe this cache of spared volumes offered just that chance.

Reading my diary entries, I could view myself from the outside looking in, just as I had examined so many defendants, consumers, and executives. In turn, I could see myself with a clarity and objectivity that I had never experienced before.

I wrote about an odd assortment of paramours—a teenage wizard, a Ghanaian bishop, and a transvestite—as well as spiritual quests in all manner of venues: a hilltop Hindu convent, a Hogwarts style psychic college, a guru's apartment in Beverly Hills. My full spectrum of experiences exposed as many secrets as a spy novel. I relished that. But more important, they provided a trail of clues leading to my ultimate destiny.

I had achieved some of the milestones of adulthood—college degrees, home ownership, and steady employment. But one accomplishment remained spectacularly out of reach: marriage and children.

"Maybe your karmic destiny in this lifetime has nothing to do with the marital vow," one friend observed. "Maybe it's pursuing another kind of vow."

As I read my journal entries, I saw how each success, each defeat, each challenge helped to define that "other vow"—maybe the reason I was born.

I hope you'll join me on this journey. Call it an archaeological dig. Perhaps it will encourage you to unravel your own secrets and to find your own divine path.

Chapter 1

JACKKNIFED

I woke up folded in half.

I struggled to orient myself. This wasn't a dream, I was almost sure. As my eyes adjusted to the dim light, I scanned the room, at least as much as I could see from my scrunched position. A spare bedroom in the bungalow where my brother, Peter, lived, buried in the hills of LA's Laurel Canyon, it was more an abandoned storage room than a cozy guest retreat. Ivy grew through the cracks in the dirty windows. A low slanted ceiling explained the throbbing bump on my head. And the spare twin bed, wheeled out from an alcove, had obviously been folded up for quite some time.

"Peter! Help! I'm stuck!" I yelled.

Peter's German shepherd ambled in. She studied me for a moment. Then she pressed her cold nose to my side, to offer encouragement.

"Nicky, go get Peter."

A trained guard dog, she dutifully obliged.

Peter arrived, coffee mug in hand. "Whatever's wrong?" He laughed, relishing the sight of his sister stuck in a bed sandwich. Throughout the night, the bed had slowly returned to its original folded position.

"Let me outta here!"

"Come on, Laur," he said, as he released me. I liked it when he used my nickname, but warm familial support probably wouldn't save me. My position could very well reflect my future. I'd fail to clear a curve and end up like the tractor trailer I'd seen jackknifed at the side of the road on my trek up the coast to LA.

The previous day—August 13, 1986—I'd abandoned the blue skies, glistening ocean, and relaxed lifestyle of "Sandy Ego" to live in a city filled with traffic jams, air pollution, ruthless Hollywood ethics, and competition from some of the most attractive and talented people in the world.

Whatever for?

"Your problem is that you're drowning in a sea of nebulousness," one friend suggested.

It was true. Nothing in San Diego gelled. Not romance. Not career. Not financial stability. By contrast, my brother's life had shot like a meteorite toward his goals—employment as a cinematographer on major motion pictures, engagement to a beautiful blonde, and homeownership, all by the age of twenty-nine. My life had trundled down the road like an oxcart, stalled by potholes and more than a ditch or two. To add insult to injury, I was three years older than my brother!

Every few months I visited Peter. Over one long holiday weekend, when I had more time to study my surroundings, I noticed there was nothing nebulous, nothing half-assed, about the City of Angels. It was all funk and punk, glitz and glamour. It felt like the solution to my nebulous life.

I wasn't willing to make the move until I saw the film *Body Heat*, a murder thriller starring Kathleen Turner. Her husband describes a former business partner as the guy who "wasn't willing to do what was necessary. And I mean whatever was necessary."

You know how some lyrics replay over and over in your head? Well, that's what happened with that bit of dialogue. I didn't want to be that guy, the guy unwilling to do whatever was necessary.

I knew what I wanted—love, career, and a connection to God. How I'd accomplish that was less clear. But one thing I *did* know, or at least strongly suspected: Sandy Ego was not on the route to my goals.

So, if moving to LA led to a jackknife or two, then so be it. I was willing to pay the price.

Chapter 2

WHITE PICKET FENCE

The next morning, I woke up to a face full of kisses. Nicky, my brother's dog, had taken a liking to me after our hike the previous afternoon. She had slept on my bed, a welcome weight, apparently, as I lay flat, rather than folded.

As a trained attack dog, Nicky would serve as both companion and protector while my brother shot a movie in Fiji for three months. In exchange for free rent, I would housesit his hillside bungalow and take care of his dog. Yes, I would have preferred my brother's company and moral support as I adjusted to LA, but my own house in the woods, along with a canine companion . . . well, that was a pretty nice alternative.

After breakfast, I shooed Nicky off the bed so I could lay out my job interview outfit. If any outfit impressed, this one would. I admired the bright blue suit with its gold buttons and pleated skirt. It was both stylish and businesslike. And the patent leather heels were high enough to be sexy but not so high that I would fall down face-first in HR.

Thanks to the writing portfolio I'd created in San Diego, an employment agency had booked interviews for what seemed like glamour jobs, in market research at a movie studio and in copywriting at an ad agency.

In the lobby of the film studio, I sat quietly, gripping a new leather portfolio I'd bought to hold my resume and a few writing samples. I dug in my purse for a lozenge. My throat was scratchy from air pollution, which was particularly bad, I'd been told, in the dead of August.

Staff passed through the lobby, studying me out of the corners of their eyes. They wore tight, low-slung jeans; tank tops displaying impressive tattoos and tans; and long, dangly earrings, accentuating graceful necks. By comparison, I looked like a librarian.

An HR assistant escorted me to a small back office. The lozenge hadn't done the trick, and I started coughing again.

"Let me get you some water," the assistant offered and darted out.

She returned with glass in hand.

"Thank you so much. I just have a little tickle in my throat."

I dabbed my sweaty brow with a Kleenex and tried to regain my composure. But the more I coughed, the more I couldn't stop coughing. Instead of "Can I live in LA?," maybe the more apt question was "Can I breathe in LA?"

I sat alone for ten, twenty, thirty, then forty minutes.

After an hour, I stole out of the back office. I had my answer. My services were not needed. People had warned me about how ruthless Hollywood could be. Now I'd experienced it firsthand. Tinseltown had initiated me.

I shot past the reception desk and punched the elevator button repeatedly to hasten my exit. As the elevator's doors closed, I yelled, "Your loss!" No one heard. But my rebuke made me feel better.

My second interview was at a mid-Wilshire ad agency. I could redeem myself. The firm's focus on health care sounded more interesting than, say, auto parts or mattresses. But I was open to any job that would build my writing portfolio. In time, I could be pickier and write about what really interested me, alternative health and spirituality.

My interviewer had been blessed with the perfect corporate face—pretty, without being distractingly beautiful—and the perfect expression: an "I will do as I am told" blankness. No idiosyncrasy or recalcitrance threatened her carriage of duty.

She didn't waste time with small talk. "We need a copywriter for Nature's Bounty, a vitamin manufacturer. Can you write copy to move those vitamins off the shelf?"

I assured her I was just the ticket, although I wondered if I had it in me to make vitamins A, B, and C dance off the page.

She gave me a penetrating look, obviously as unconvinced as I. "Pardon me if I'm being presumptuous, but you seem like an altruist, not the hard-driving persuader we're looking for."

Wow, good call, Blank Face.

As we sat in silence perusing each other, I heard what sounded like clanking glass. A silver trolley, stocked with bottles and tumblers, rolled down the hall.

"Oh, this is 'Martini Friday,'" she explained. "One of our clients is a distiller who delivers varieties of gin and other liquors for us to try."

"Interesting," I sputtered.

"We're party animals here," she said dispassionately. "Are you?"

"I can be," I said, realizing that "party animal" probably meant more than a martini on a Friday afternoon.

I punched the elevator button for the ground level. Would I ever be hip and happening enough for LA? It wasn't looking good.

The employment agency didn't give up on me. The next day, it sent me on a temporary assignment: helping a Russian in West Hollywood edit his "business" book.

When Oleg opened his apartment door, I wondered if I should run for it while I had the chance. He looked like Dracula, with slicked-back black hair, deep-set black eyes, and an all-black ensemble. His studio was smoke-filled and dim, with a single bulb burning overhead. But I needed the $25-per-hour wage, so I gingerly stepped inside and accepted his offer of a glass of orange juice.

From the looks of his spare quarters, it was obvious that Oleg couldn't afford even a few hours of my time. So, over the next three months, I met with him weekly, one hour "on the clock" to discuss my edits and another hour for socializing.

He served caviar and butter sandwiches on Wonder Bread, and we shared stories about our lives. At twenty-eight, Oleg had abandoned his widowed mother and girlfriend ("a true Slavic beauty") to make a better life in LA. He'd defected from Russia over the Yugoslavian mountains with only a toothbrush and bottle of vodka in his breast pocket.

Now he was alone, more alone than I'd ever been. He held up the insect he'd befriended, a cockroach that lived under his oven. "Count the sections. Count the legs. It is beautiful animal."

He hoped to make $5,000 a month selling his get-rich-quick book, aptly titled *How to Make $5,000 a Month at Home.*

When Oleg asked about me, I demurred. "Oh, Oleg, my story can't compare to yours. I drove my Toyota Corolla from a small town in Ohio called Gates Mills, 2,400 miles across the country to San Diego. I lived there for twelve years and moved to LA a few weeks ago. I didn't hike across the mountains with a bottle of vodka in my breast pocket."

"Gates Mills? Where's that?"

"Oh, it's a village nestled in a river valley outside Cleveland, filled with white picket fences."

"Picket fence?" he asked, pronouncing it *peekeet venz*. "What *peekeet*?"

"It's vertical slats of wood, connected by horizontal slats."

Oleg nodded, rolling an unlit cigarette between his fingers, as he contemplated the mystery of the picket.

"The white picket fence is a symbol of having achieved the American dream."

"Which is?" Oleg asked, genuinely curious.

"Your freestanding house in the suburbs, with two cars in the garage, a chicken in the pot, a little boy and girl playing with their dog in the backyard, surrounded by . . ."

"A vite peekeet venz," Oleg said, finishing my sentence.

We laughed. I needn't have worried that my story fell short on intrigue.

"Did you find dream?" he asked.

"No, that's why I moved to LA, to pursue my own dream."

"Which is?"

"I don't know yet. I'm in the process of creating it."

He nodded. If anyone understood what I meant, Oleg did. He made me realize there were others like me, probably thousands, who didn't fit in where they grew up and who'd moved to LA to find their place in the world.

We'd been taught to hate each other during the Cold War, yet Oleg and I slowly became kindred spirits, bonding over our attempt to flourish in a strange, new city. Maybe there was no niche for us back in Moscow or Cleveland, but surely LA offered some place to find our tribe, to ply our skills, to fulfill our callings.

I was happy to keep listening to Oleg's fascinating tales, but as the weeks wore on, I noticed changes. First, he became rude. When I showed up sporting new eyeglasses—the large octagonal frames in vogue at the time—he blurted, "You might as well wear scuba mask!" He took down his beloved Elvis Presley poster, replacing it with a small photo of the Kremlin, "to remind myself of where party leaders decide how Russian people should lead their lives." And his skin took on a yellowish cast.

To make matters worse, Oleg had caught on that *How to Make $5,000 a Month at Home* probably was not going to do that for him or any reader. If only I'd edited it better, he chastised me, then maybe it would have achieved success. Boxes of self-published books stood waist-high in the corner. He'd significantly overestimated demand.

He started serving our caviar sandwiches with vodka shots instead of our usual orange juice. Clinking my glass, Oleg would down a shot, then suck on a pickle. He'd repeat this process in rapid succession, while I nursed my first round.

I began to view Oleg as a transplanted tree, dying in its new soil. Burying his past and trying to adapt to a wildly different culture proved too much of a shock.

As his company began to drain me, our weekly visits became biweekly, then monthly, then canceled altogether. Eventually, I lost touch with him. *I'll never find out what happens to Oleg.* At least that's what I figured at the time.

Chapter 3

LEISURE SUIT LARRY

I transferred my gym membership from San Diego to its sister studio in LA. After a rousing aerobics class, I headed for the indoor Jacuzzi. My vision blurred by the steam and absence of eyeglasses, I slid into the bubbling water, shoulder-to-shoulder with another member—a man with long hair and silky skin. He was a hand model from South Dakota named Lance.

Lulled by the warm water, he delivered his life philosophy: "I don't think, I just act."

On a date the following week, I discovered his bromide translated to minimal conversation and lots of sexual advances. True, Lance's hands were beautiful—large, sculpted, and graceful. And there was the matter of his exceptional skin. But I could see those gifts might not prove enough to keep me coming back for more. Still, I felt Angeleno-ed by the experience. Isn't that what Angelenos did? Date hand models they met in the gym Jacuzzi?

One afternoon, as I hiked the Hollywood Hills with my canine companion, a man stopped to pet Nicky. "He's so well behaved," he marveled, as Nicky obediently sat and stoically accepted his caresses.

"He thanks you."

"By the way, my name's Reed."

"Nice to meet you. This is Nicky, and I'm Laurie."

"Hope to see you again," Reed said, as he headed in the opposite direction.

We chatted regularly on our walks, until one day, on the eve of his business trip, I offered to feed his fish.

"That would be great," he said.

The next day I dropped by to retrieve directions about the fish food that Reed had left with the key under his doormat. Like many men's apartments, his one-bedroom looked makeshift. There was the round Ikea rug, not big enough to cover the scuffed parquet floor. There was the straw sombrero hat hung on the dining room wall, no doubt a girlfriend's stab at "brightening up the place." And a monochromatic color scheme, save for a sapphire blue fish hiding in the corner of the aquarium. The whole scene cried out, "Take me with you. Can't you see I need a proper home?"

Upon his return, to thank me, he invited me to breakfast. I suggested bowling instead, at an alley called Pinz, midway between our houses.

"Where should we meet?" I asked. "At the shoes?"

"Too smelly," he said.

"The cocktail lounge?"

"Too Tarantino."

"The video arcade?"

"How old are you anyway?"

"The bowling ball polishing machine?"

"We don't want to go there."

Finally, we agreed to meet at the alley's diner. Our conversation over omelets did not match our earlier repartee. He seemed a little pinched. Still, I didn't rule him out as a romantic prospect. And he seemed equally hopeful. After breakfast, he invited me back to his apartment "to show me something."

He had just purchased a video game called *Leisure Suit Larry*. "The point is to get Larry laid," Reed explained.

"I see," I said, wondering where he was going with this train of thought.

Tapping the arrow keys, he directed Larry to approach a woman sitting at a bar. Larry said hi, and she slapped him. "No matter what I do, I never get anywhere with the ladies at the bar," Reed lamented. "Like in real life," he added.

I could understand why. His overshare on our first date gave me the creeps. "Hey, I better get going," I said, quickly collecting my purse and jacket. "Thank you for breakfast." Then I turned on my heels and fled.

After that encounter, Nicky and I stopped running into Reed on the trails. That was for the best.

A few weeks after our breakfast, I got a cryptic call at 2:30 a.m. Half asleep, I answered the phone. Someone breathed heavily into the receiver, without saying anything.

"Reed, is that you?"

He laughed and hung up. This was before caller ID, so I couldn't track who'd called. But based on the *Leisure Suit Larry* incident, I suspected Reed might play such a prank.

The next night, I got a second mysterious call.

"Hi," the caller said timidly.

Right away I knew it wasn't Reed.

"Oh, my God, you're an obscene phone caller, aren't you?"

"Yes," he admitted.

"How did you get my number?"

"Just dialing randomly."

"But what do you hope to accomplish?"

He didn't answer.

Over subsequent late-night calls, I learned that his name was Matt and that he had jet-black hair to his waist. Despite being a high school dropout, he was intelligent and self-reflective.

"I'm nutty, Laurie. And impulsive. And dependent."

Those words sounded like therapy-speak. Hopefully, he was still seeing a professional.

For the next three months, he called two or three times a week. I'd begun to look forward to our exchanges.

He shared his experiences with women. "Sometimes, when the chemistry is right, good things start to happen in both our lives—jobs, projects, windfalls of some sort. It's like we're feeding each other in ways we could never do on our own. That's how you know a relationship works. It makes you more than who you were."

I admitted that had rarely, if ever, happened to me.

"You feed me emotionally, Laurie," he said quietly. "And vice versa."

What an odd thing for one's mystery caller to say. But he was right. Matt fed me emotionally. Since he'd started calling, my skin had gotten clearer. I didn't reach for my Xanax as much. And I felt energized the day after talking to him.

Eventually, though, Matt stopped calling or, in today's vernacular, he ghosted me. Just as well, I consoled myself. What future did I have with an obscene phone caller? He was simply a mythical creature who'd flown in my window one night to deliver a lesson or two. Too often, and this fact was hard to admit, men made my life worse. Romances yielded distractions, roller-coaster rides or just plain drains. Not Matt. He'd let me experience the emotional reciprocity, the synergistic betterment I craved in a relationship. Then, the deed done, he'd flown away.

Chapter 4

THE FAR SIDE

I yearned to plant roots in LA—to build a circle of friends, find a steady job I loved, and create a romance that had potential. Instead, I'd fallen down a rabbit hole. I'd met intriguing characters—Blank Face, the Russian defector, and an obscene phone caller. They'd taught me a thing or two, to be sure. But none had led to terra firma. Maybe if I focused on normal forms of recreation, normal forms of "putting myself out there," I'd find what I was looking for.

One day, I decided to walk Nicky closer to home, on the sun-dappled back roads of Laurel Canyon with the hope of meeting a neighbor or two. Immediately, though, I saw I'd made a big mistake. When the neighborhood dogs spotted a German shepherd through the slats of their backyard fences, they growled, rammed their snouts through holes in the wood, and tried to jump over their enclosures. Nicky responded in kind. Perhaps my neighbors' dogs instinctively knew a killer attack dog when they saw one. Hell, they were probably killer attack dogs themselves. In 1969, Charles Manson's family had gone on a killing spree just a few miles away. Many residents bought attack dogs after that.

I returned home so breathless and stressed, I skipped my morning coffee. While I loved to cuddle in bed with Nicky and feel her back pressed against mine at night, I had to remember Peter had sent Nicky to Berlin to train as an attack dog. She was both a friend and a loaded shotgun.

Maybe a few hours at the gym would be relaxing. While the layout of the fitness center in Hollywood mirrored its San Diego branch, the signage proved markedly different. A laminated sign at the reception desk read: PLEASE KEEP YOUR CLOTHES ON AT ALL TIMES. A sign in the ladies' room followed a similar line of thought: DO NOT DYE YOUR HAIR IN THIS SINK.

Afraid I'd run into Lance in the Jacuzzi, I took the elevator to the sundeck on the roof. There I stretched out in my navy Speedo one-piece bathing suit. What a perfect way to spend an afternoon. But as I dug into my novel, I couldn't help but notice my fellow sunbathers. More than one had ignored the sign at the front desk. The women were so well-endowed, I figured they must be porn stars. The most prolific porn production in the world took place just over the hill in the San Fernando Valley. If anyone needed a full body tan, it was a porn star.

To add to the drama, a few men parked atop a three-story billboard called out, "Looking good, girls! Why don't you take it all off?"

They sat scrunched on the billboard's catwalk, the size of a tiny front porch. The sign promoted Xtronx's Winkies: blinking computer chips, a gag gift, similar to the pet rock, that was all the rage at the time.

I shrugged my shoulders at one sunbather. "Who the heck are they?"

"Oh, they're participating in a contest sponsored by a local radio station," she explained. "Whoever lives on the billboard the longest wins a Ferrari. They've been camped up there for months."

"Are we their only form of entertainment?"

"I'm afraid so," she said, rearranging her ample bosom for maximum exposure.

I gave the contestants a halfhearted wave and returned to my book. I couldn't concentrate, though, so I laid my head back on the chaise lounge and closed my eyes. But the contestants' taunts—"Come on, take it off! Take off your suit!"—made dozing impossible.

The next week, I signed up for a tennis clinic sponsored by a local rec center. What could be more normal than improving one's backhand?

As tennis ball machines delivered a relentless stream of volleys, a coach critiqued my form and that of my ten or so classmates. Then, once a month, the center hosted a tennis tournament. The clinic's participants—mostly teens and their parents—invited their large extended families to root for them from the bleachers. When I hit a ball into the net, their cheers angered me, but also spurred me to play better.

I tried to fit in with my fellow athletes, investing in mid-thigh tennis dresses like theirs and adopting teen slang like "You crushed it!" But nothing I did could change my odd-man-out status. I was a good fifteen years older than my teenage classmates, and fifteen years younger than their parents. The rec center served families, not singles like me.

Midway through a class on how to return a lob, I decided to stop for a break.

"Are you leaving?" the pro asked.

"No, Coach, just taking a breather, a little walk."

Turning away, I heard him mutter under his breath, "Yeah, on the far side."

The guy was perceptive. As I walked around the perimeter of

the rec center, I thought about what had led to my current life "on the far side."

I attended a men's liberal arts college smack dab in the middle of the Ohio cornfields. After 150 years as an all-male institution, the college trustees and alumni reluctantly agreed to accept women. I'd joined the first co-ed class to graduate since the school's founding in 1824. The trouble was the kind of woman who attended one of the oldest formerly all-male colleges in the country was quite different from her male counterpart. Not surprisingly, she tended to be more unconventional.

Still, I reveled in the stability, the this-is-the-way-we've-always-done-it vibe that permeated the campus. After all, I was the daughter of a Cleveland banker who also served as mayor of my tiny hometown of Gates Mills. Stability was part of my DNA. But all the while, I tried to overlook the fact that my gender happened to be *not* the way the school had always done it.

After I graduated in 1974, I moved in with my mother and stepfather, who'd relocated from Ohio to San Diego a few years earlier.

Bonded by our love of art—my mother, as an interior designer; my stepfather, as an architect; and I, as a studio art major—we got along effortlessly. They welcomed me into their hilltop home overlooking the ocean until I got on my feet financially.

I tried my hand at different occupations—a year each as a clerk typist on a naval base, a pharmacy technician at a children's hospital, and a litigation paralegal at a real estate law firm. A market research job at an ad agency looked promising, until I discovered a full one-third of the staff had been "hired" as unpaid interns. The combination of thousands of students studying at San Diego's many colleges and the local economy's dearth of creative jobs paved the way for lots of free labor. Those who were paid like me—at a whopping $8 per hour—couldn't expect many raises or much upward mobility, either.

Getting on my feet financially proved more challenging than I, or my parents, had anticipated. I continually hit a dead end.

Chapter 5

LUNAR MADNESS

In 1976, a couple of years after I moved to San Diego, a college friend introduced me to her next-door neighbor. Twenty-one, six-foot-four, with pale green eyes and sun-streaked hair, Miles definitely qualified as a hunk. When I met him at the front door of his family home near the beach, I was so startled by his good looks, I could barely navigate the screen door he opened for me.

He lived rent-free in his mother's back garage, while his three younger siblings resided in the front house. For pocket money, he served as a handyman for his mother's investment properties. But other than the occasional plumbing or roofing task, his life revolved around play: batting a sponge ball back and forth with a parrot who'd flown in his window one day; duking it out with friends over bridge and chess; and partaking in amazingly strong Thai stick. But his greatest love was his band, Lunar Madness, which played at a local dive bar.

I dutifully attended his shows, watching the audience hoot and holler, chanting, "Lu-nar-Maaaad-nessss," pumping their fists in the air with each syllable. After the band's set, guests stormed my corner table to buy Lunar Madness T-shirts.

I marveled at Miles's lack of domesticity, as did my parents. "I can always tell when Miles has been here," my stepfather observed. "The paintings are always slightly askew." Like a puppy who hadn't developed full coordination, Miles failed to clear the walls while walking through the rooms and corridors of my parents' home.

When I visited Miles, I'd have to slowly scan the garage. He often napped at all hours (usually after a spot of Thai stick), and his quarters were in such disarray that I could miss his form stretched out wherever sleep had overtaken him. I quickly understood why high school classmates had signed his yearbook "To the Sandman's best customer."

In his makeshift kitchen, he ate like a child left to his own devices. At a local big-box store, he bought a foot-high stack of corn tortillas and a ten-pound hunk of cheese. Breakfast, lunch, and dinner consisted of a quesadilla or two, washed down with a can of Mountain Dew.

In keeping with his childlike persona, Miles orchestrated all manner of pranks. While the couple next door ate dinner in their kitchen just a few feet from his garage, we timed how long it took to stop their conversation. Feigning raucous lovemaking and calling out "No, please, Miles, please don't bite me!" proved particularly effective.

And after he convinced me to buy my first answering machine, he left a message that absorbed all sixty minutes of the audiocassette, reciting an entire book of Wordsworth's poetry.

As my twenty-third birthday gift, Miles painted a twelve-foot mural of me in the nude, on the garage wall, replete with drilled holes so the reclining figure could wear tortoise shell glasses like mine.

Peter Pan personified, Miles lived completely in the pleasure of the moment, with no worry of the future. His approach to life allowed me to play Peter Pan, too, or at least Wendy. Instinctively, I knew that in my early twenties, I was too unformed to embrace an adult institution like marriage. Serving as Peter Pan's accomplice worked just fine for me.

Then one night, two years into our relationship, after multiple hits off his bong, Miles asked me to marry him. But his proposal sounded more like a business proposition when he added the caveat: "You'd have to downsize, of course."

"You mean sleep on the cement floor of your mother's garage?" I asked, my usual diplomacy blunted by inebriation equal to Miles's.

"Yeah, if you really loved me, you'd do that," he shot back.

"What if I want more? Or would you set the standard for how we'd live?"

"Well, yeah, I'm the *guy*."

"So, be it castle or hovel, I'd have to follow suit as your wife?"

"Yep."

Why had I never seen this chauvinistic side of Miles before?

"Forget about living arrangements." Growing more sober by the minute, I decided it best to change the subject. "What about doing something with your talents? I know you've got Lunar Madness, but what about something that makes money? After all, your high school *did* place you in its gifted program."

"But I'm already gifted. I don't need to do anything."

"No, that designation means you have all the more responsibility to apply your gifts. I mean, why would I tie my future to a man who squanders his talents?"

As I drove home, discombobulated by our frank exchange, I realized I loved Miles the way Wendy loved Peter Pan. I relished his never growing up, playing with no guilt, oblivious to what the future might hold. I *didn't* love him like a woman who wished to tie her destiny to his, to bear his children, to run his household, to try (and most likely fail) to motivate him to make something of his life.

I suspected if we married, I would slowly adopt Miles's exceedingly laid-back lifestyle. His inertia would become my inertia.

Society had so drummed into my head *You need a man to complete you* that it never occurred to me the opposite might occur. Fortunately, this young romance set the record straight: a man could just as easily deplete me.

After I turned down Miles's proposal, we drifted apart. I still sold Lunar Madness T-shirts at his gig that summer. But I was glad we'd parted ways. I suspected the man I knew at twenty-three would remain the same man at sixty-three—an eternal Peter Pan.

Chapter 6

PEA GREEN

I encouraged Miles to take advantage of his God-given talents. But what about myself? Talk about the pot calling the kettle black. So, at twenty-six, I launched what would become a lifelong spiritual quest. Starting out, I wanted to learn how to talk to God. Maybe that would help me access my calling.

My upbringing had included a spot of religion. But that experience revealed more of the comical than the transcendent side of church. It gave me no clue about how to connect with God.

Every Sunday, my parents dropped off my brother, Peter, and me at an austere, white-steepled Episcopal church along the banks of the Chagrin River, in our hometown of Gates Mills, Ohio. They believed children should be exposed to religion, even if they themselves personally did not subscribe to it. In Sunday school, held in the church's cold basement, I won a roll of Lifesavers for correctly reciting the chapters of the New Testament. But when I painted Jesus pea green on a church banner, my teacher reprimanded me. "Jesus isn't green," she explained, trying to hide her anger.

Peter, an altar boy at the 11 a.m. service, told me what the pastor wore under his ministerial robes. After each service, the reverend yanked his gown over his head to reveal bright white tennis shorts and polo shirt. Considering the minister's pedestrian sermon and perfunctory handshakes with parishioners, we agreed that his afternoon tennis matches, at the country club across the street, served as the real highlight of his Sundays.

In my twenties, I began experimenting with a different denomination every Sunday. One week, at the Church of Religious Science near my house, a pretty blonde charismatic named Teri led a congregation so large, she hosted Sunday morning services at a convention hall in downtown San Diego. The hall marquis read: MAKE A TOUCHDOWN FOR GOD. True to the sign, her sermon sounded like a locker-room pep talk prior to an NFL game. The choir sang, "Smile, smile, smile," while a slideshow featured smiling faces. At the end of the service, we all held hands and wished our seat partners "the best week of your life!" Video cameras whirled on all sides, capturing Teri's sermon in case you wanted to buy a VHS tape in the lobby after the service.

When I hit thirty, I decided a Zen temple might suit me better. It was tucked away in a leafy neighborhood near San Diego's Balboa Park. In a quieter venue, I stood a better chance of looking within. My girlfriend Zani and I arrived just as the Zen master hit the gong signaling the start of a two-hour meditation. Zani and I wore matching over-the-knee boots that had to be left at the door. As Zani loudly unzipped her right boot, I realized we'd worn the wrong footwear to the temple.

"Shh, Zani, come on!" I slowly unzipped my boots to minimize the sound. To rile me, Zani yanked the rest of the zipper with a sudden jerk, making an even more pronounced sound.

I pressed my index finger to my lips, but it was too late. The zipping had echoed through the silent foyer. We fell to the floor in gales of giggles. The Zen master appeared, shoved us out the back door, and, for good measure, threw our boots after us.

"How Zen was that?"

"Not very," Zani replied, no longer laughing.

We retrieved our boots scattered on the lawn and headed to our car in silence. We'd failed as Buddhist devotees before we'd even entered the temple chambers.

A more traditional denomination, like the Church of Jesus Christ of Latter-day Saints, I figured, might be more welcoming. But after the service, five ushers in black suits escorted me to a back office. I was obviously not a member of the fold.

"Who *are* you?" they demanded.

Who was I? Exactly. But apparently, I was not going to answer that question at a Mormon temple.

"Honey, maybe you need to talk to someone," my mother suggested.

"I guess," I said meekly.

She booked an appointment with a therapist named Barbara who saw clients on the top floor of an old Victorian mansion in a nearby tree-lined neighborhood of San Diego.

Despite the lovely setting, things did not go well with Barbara. She opened each session with "So what are you feeling right now?"

I'd hold up my palm facing her. "Give me a sec," I'd say. "Let me think."

"No, I don't want you to think. I just want you to tell me how you feel."

"Unmoored?"

"That's not a feeling word."

"Clueless?"

"Not a feeling word either."

This exchange went on for the first ten minutes of each of our \$100 sessions, until one day she declared, "You know what your problem is, Laurie? You don't have a feeling vocabulary."

That conclusion didn't sound good. But one thing was for sure: I wouldn't be developing one in my weekly sessions with Barbara.

Certainly, I had been resourceful in my efforts to gain traction in some aspects of my life. But I had to admit I was getting nowhere fast. While trying on heels at Macy's, I turned to my mother for guidance. "What's wrong with me, Mom? Why aren't I getting anywhere in my life?"

"Honey," she said, wrapping her arm around my shoulder. "You're just a late bloomer."

That, I agreed, described me to a tee. I had not found my person, or my tribe for that matter. I had not found my occupation or my religion. Yes, I had not yet bloomed. But I was beginning to wonder, would I *ever* bloom?

Chapter 7

GREAT EXPECTATIONS

Until I learned how to access God's will for me, I resorted to a more earthbound source of insight: a career counselor. So what if she looked fifteen; maybe she could identify my calling. Based on the results of my personality and interest assessments, she suggested a career as a writer, concentrating on business to maximize my income.

Immediately, I set out to build a portfolio of writing samples, submitting stories to local weeklies. When *San Diego Woman* agreed to print my piece, on the cover no less, I skipped up and down my apartment. I had never been more pleased in my life.

I slipped each published story into a clear plastic sheath, collected in a leather notebook, the best sold at the local art supply store. Then, in 1985, that portfolio helped me to escape San Diego and land my first full-time job in LA. After I worked for Oleg on his get-rich-quick book, a business publisher hired me as a copy editor, at $15 per hour, nearly double my previous wage.

When Peter returned from his film shoot in Fiji, I started hunting for an apartment. In short order, I snagged a rent-controlled one-bedroom in Palms for $610 a month. Yeah, it was sad to say goodbye to Nicky and I would have liked to hang out with Peter as his housemate. Still, I loved my new digs. I decorated it with prints from David Hockney's swimming pool series, brightening my walls with coral, turquoise, and grass green. My favorite flowered quilt, now well-worn, covered a vintage brass bed. Before rising every morning, I marveled at the three palm trees outside my third-floor window filled with chattering birds.

I built a circle of friends from work—the receptionist and two fellow copy editors—who almost compensated for my lack of a special someone.

Nonetheless, after a few months at my new job, I developed a strange malaise: a low-level nausea and fatigue. Doctors couldn't figure out what was wrong. Blood tests found little. X-rays revealed no answers either.

Finally, I booked an appointment with the head of infectious diseases at UCLA Medical Center. Maybe I'd contracted a rare tropical disease while vacationing in a tiny town in Mexico. Five minutes and $300 later, the doctor declared, "You're depressed," and wrote a prescription for Prozac.

Really? Maybe I was a little depressed. As of late, "putting myself out there" had netted a type A art dealer who couldn't stop talking and a professor who rarely talked. My male colleagues at work were courtly, handsome, perceptive writers, but also gay, married, or too young. Exasperation, not depression, was my most pressing emotion. Had science developed a pill for that?

I threw away my bottle of antidepressants and spent $2,000 on a membership to Great Expectations, the video dating service that was all the rage in the 1980s. Maybe a man would solve my ennui. And not just any man. An investment of two grand meant the men I'd meet would be serious about a relationship. No players or commitment-phobes would join.

On Saturday afternoons, I visited the "library." There, members sat in silence, earnestly paging through loose-leaf notebooks filled with five thousand members' photos and bios. Each profile included a member's height, weight, religion, smoking status, interests, and a thumbnail of their ideal mate. In a small viewing booth, I watched stacks of VHS tapes that featured interviews with members I'd chosen from the notebooks.

One time I snuck my own tape into the booth to see how I looked to the men. The dating service's mandated makeup artist, hair stylist, and videographer had transformed me into a creature I could not recognize. In my three-minute, on-camera interview, I looked like a poodle fresh from the groomer, eager for a pat on the head.

I sent handwritten notes to the men I culled from the VHS tapes. Then, a few days later, I girded myself and called an 800 phone number to discover whether the attraction was mutual. After I punched in my membership number, a robotic voice came on the line: *You have chosen Member #36284 and his answer is:* (long pause) *No, thank you.* Or: *Yes, thank you. His phone number is . . .*

One Friday evening, after two no-thank-you responses, I called my coworker Denise in tears. Even though she held the lowest position at work—as the publisher's front-desk receptionist—she was the wisest on staff.

"I just got spurned by a robot," I said, explaining the dating service's rejection system. I went on to describe what bothered me even more. Our colleague Leo, a twenty-three-year-old writer who shared an office with me, had joined the service and, within a few weeks, had met the woman he planned to marry. "How come Leo found someone and I have not?" I lamented.

"It makes sense that the dating service worked for Leo," Denise observed. "He's a simple, conventional man. You, on the other hand, are complex and unique. I mean, don't you find there's a profound difference between you and other people? So, something mainstream like Great Expectations was bound to fail you."

Denise's logic made me feel better. Still, I bravely requested a spreadsheet at the dating service's front desk. A numerical code explained the reason each man turned me down. Maybe if I learned the reasons men didn't like me, I could change myself into what they wanted.

At 5'8", I frequently got Reason #13: "Too tall." Well, I wasn't going to be able to change that. But usually, men listed the far vaguer Reason #4: "Not my type." If, indeed, I fell into the "unusual" category as Denise claimed, "Not my type" would be a natural reason for turning me down. I would be hardly any man's type, whether at Great Expectations or out in the real world.

Being different feels like a precarious place to be, I wrote in my diary that night. *People want to be with their own people, their own tribe. And while I am a lot of things, I am decidedly not the same ilk as most. That means exclusion and, who knows, eventually death.*

True to Denise's characterization of the service as "mainstream," many of the men who asked me out worked in conventional professions. They were insurance brokers, tax attorneys, and optometrists. I convinced myself that these prospects were marriage material, that I should give them a try.

I did, but most dates were unmemorable, save for one with a rare creative type—an animator at Disney. Over lunch at an outdoor café, he gave me a long, penetrating look, then, leaning across the table, he whispered, "You know, if we got married, you'd have to wear rubber."

"Rubber?" I asked, wondering if this was his odd proclivity. I had visions of cooking the family dinner in a red rubber catsuit.

"Yes. I'm a vegetarian," he explained, "so you couldn't wear any animal products."

"Of course," I said, with a slow grave nod, implying my acquiescence.

But his request felt ominous, like the tip of an iceberg. Other demands—what I ate, how much I weighed, what I read—would surely follow. I had barely fashioned my own rules of how *I* wanted to live as a free agent, so adhering to another's set of rules felt like a hijacking of sorts.

To make matters worse, I couldn't imagine the tables turned. What if I'd asked the same of him? "As my husband, you'd have to wear rubber." Most likely his response would have been, "Check, please."

Slowly, I began to hibernate. I made it to my job, but little else. I stopped "putting myself out there" and hunkered down in my third-floor apartment.

On weekends, I'd draw the curtains, blocking out the bright blue skies and swaying palms. I read memoirs penned by authors who lived on the margins of society, like banished royals and call girls. I feverishly journaled at least a dozen pages a day, dedicating a shelf to a growing line of multicolored, hardbound diaries. My viewing fare fell into what friends referred to as "your disaster porn"—documentaries about coups d'état, epidemics, and credit card debt, chosen, I suspect, to make me feel better about my own comparable state of affairs. But none of these diversions changed my plight. I still felt too sickly, too fragile, to venture out into the real world.

While I could manage days, nights were a challenge. Falling asleep felt like trying to put out a four-alarm fire. First, I'd pop several triple-action, time-release sleep aids of melatonin, valerian root, and skullcap. Next came yoga by candlelight, a hot shower, and light reading. Then I'd get on my knees and, leaning my elbows on my brass bed, talk to God, in the only way I could think of, like with a friend. "Hey, I'm going downhill, God. You have got to help me here. What am I missing?" I'd listen for God's answer, but it felt like trying to catch a radio station driving through a mountain pass, the signal intermittent and garbled.

If I still failed to fall asleep, I'd bring out the heavy artillery—a half-tablet of Xanax, followed by an "oh, hell, why not take the whole thing." I'd down the second half, soak in a hot bath and guzzle a bottle of cabernet.

All these inebriants eventually sickened me. I'd end up throwing up everything I'd ingested while still stretched out in the tub. In my fervor to fall asleep, I feared I'd drown, choke on my own vomit, or overdose.

In my diary, I struggled to make sense of my decline. I accepted that if the doctor at UCLA could not find anything physically wrong with me, then my malaise would have to stem from a psychological source. The only useful observation my former therapist Barbara ever made was, "You tend to somatize—internalize your emotions, stuff them back into your body."

I didn't have health insurance, nor could I afford the out-of-pocket cost of therapy. My diagnosis and treatment would have to be of the do-it-yourself variety.

I suspected that my pain emanated from something more complicated than "Gee, I'm sad." So I dragged myself to the public library one Saturday afternoon to peruse every disorder listed in the *DSM III,* the diagnostic statistical manual commonly used by therapists. When I came to the symptoms of undischarged trauma, I saw myself: poor digestion, chronic fatigue, flat affect, disengagement, and insomnia. That constellation of maladies perfectly described my malaise.

So, what was my trauma? That night in my diary, I listed the kinds of trauma that might qualify:

- *Leaving behind my family and friends in San Diego*
- *Moving to LA with little or no support system (Peter was usually out of town on a film shoot)*
- *Increasing alienation and anxiety as I dated one dud after another*
- *Deep loneliness*
- *Financial precarity*
- *Fertility deadline (time was running out if I wanted children)*
- *Finding LA's culture more kaleidoscopic than cozy, communal, and conducive to nesting*
- *Spending money I couldn't afford on Great Expectations, only to feel even more unmatchable and alone*

I had not defected from Russia like Oleg—that would have been really traumatic—but I'd still experienced trauma that needed addressing.

But how? I called my wise friend Denise for advice.

"I think your trauma comes from lovelessness," she began. "And you're not alone. So many in LA are hunting, searching, clamoring to find love."

"So true."

"But in the process, they neglect to access the very love inside them, the love stuck in their very souls. A man may or may not materialize. And even if he appears, he might not stay. He may die, find someone else, or lose interest. But you will always have yourself. Try it. Find the love within you."

"Gosh, Denise, maybe you should be a therapist, not a receptionist."

"Thanks for the vote of confidence, Laurie. But listen, gotta go. Let me know how it goes, okay?"

That night, instead of launching my prodigious course of sleep aids, I vowed to find the love within. I spread my pink childhood blanket with its frayed hem on my living room carpet. I inserted a lullaby in my audiocassette player—"When You Wish Upon a Star"—then I lay spread-eagled on my back.

I imagined God looking down at me, thinking, *What a squirmy, struggling little creature you are. But I love you anyway. Do you know that?*

I switched off the lullaby and tried to feel that divine love. After a few minutes, I was astounded. The love was stronger than I'd ever experienced. It wasn't tainted with *Is he the one?* or *Will he love me back?* It was loving on a wide, open, smooth field, with no potholes to trip me or nettles to stick me.

I called Denise the next morning. "Oh my God."

Chapter 8

OSCAR

"Denise, you opened up a part of me I didn't know was there."

"So, has this changed anything?" she asked.

"What do you mean?"

"Will you stay in seclusion or join us in the world again?"

"Not sure yet. But what I do know is that I'm onto something. What it *is* exactly, I don't know yet."

"Okay, well that sounds mysterious. Keep me posted."

After I hung up, I curled up in bed and gazed out the window overlooking palm fronds shivering in the wind. What the hell *did* happen as I lay spread-eagled on my pink blanket? Where did that intense love come from? Was it self-love, God's love, love just floating around in the ether? Or a combination of all three? I felt like I'd had a psychedelic experience that I didn't know how to integrate into my day-to-day life.

I propped pillows against my brass headboard, grabbed my lap desk, and opened my diary. Maybe journaling would help me make sense of things. I launched a stream-of-consciousness entry:

> *Butchy* [my eighty-eight-year-old grandfather, who lived to ninety-eight] *once asked, "Are you a weak girl?" What the context was, I can't remember. But his question reflected his gotta-be-tough approach to life. I shot back, "No, Butchy, I'm a strong girl!" For the past six months, living in isolation, I proved I was strong. I can live on my own, without a boyfriend, without a husband, without a roommate. But the loneliness has been intense, sickeningly intense. I suspect it has caused my insomnia. And, if sustained too much longer, I can predict with certainty that it will precipitate illness, maybe even disease. I know that sounds like an exaggeration. But I know deep in my bones, it's true. I used to think marriage and children would be nice, a goal, but not an imperative. Now, though, after experiencing the dire consequences of aloneness, marriage feels more like a life-and-death matter. I don't want to die, and I'm sure I might if I live alone too much longer.*

Certainly, dating up to that point had not yielded the kind of companionship I yearned for. And my neighbors didn't exactly whet my appetite for more courtship. A single mom next door slammed her phone against our shared wall during fights with her baby papa. And the husband in the adjoining complex, after a rumpus with his wife, would take off down the street in his convertible, then back up in wide zigzags to deliver one last invective. After a particularly vicious exchange that almost came to blows, I called out, "Do you want the police to be called?"

The husband caught my gaze as I leaned over my third-floor balcony. "Lady, this is LA!" he barked, as if what I was witnessing was business as usual in the City of Angels. *Get over it.*

Returning to bed, I thought, *Love can be a battlefield. Am I prepared to reenter the fray?*

Soon after, Oscar, my neighbor's black cat, helped me answer that question. He padded across the railing of our adjoining balconies, slunk through my balcony door, hopped up on my kitchen counter, and lapped up the milk in my bowl of shredded wheat. He explored every square inch of my apartment, taking particular interest in a philodendron, which he gnawed on for a minute. Finally, he grazed my calf and purred, as if to say, *Hey girl, it's been fun. But gotta go.* Then he ambled out the balcony door and disappeared.

From then on, I kept the sliding door to my balcony open six inches—wide enough for Oscar to squeeze through. At Petco, I bought a variety pack of cat toys—catnip fish, mice, and balls—and collected them in a basket near the open door. *Oh, how he'll love to bat them around my living room carpet,* I marveled.

The smell of catnip, however, did not entice him back. So, one Saturday afternoon, I marched over to my neighbor's apartment to ask if Oscar could come over to play. Before I knocked, I pressed my ear against the doorframe. Maybe I could hear her cat's signature purr. But I could not. I hesitated, then turned away. My invitation probably was not such a good idea. She'd view me as a catnapper.

After a few weeks, I accepted the cold truth—Oscar's impromptu visit had been a one-time event. But his short appearance had delivered a lesson. He'd shown me how much I craved connection—not just feline, but divine and human, too.

Chapter 9

PURPLE PERSON

Oscar reminded me of the cozy domesticity I was missing in my hibernation. Yes, I could get my own cat. But a cat *and* a man sounded better. I'd canceled my $2,000-per-year account at Great Expectations. It had proved fruitless. Instead, I joined a chat room called Talk Channel. Even if it didn't yield a boyfriend, hopefully it would provide some much-needed human interaction and an escape from my seclusion.

I could access the chat room on the newfangled technology called BBS, an electronic bulletin board system that would evolve into the global internet. I chose Perfect Stranger as my handle. Unlike in real life, in the darkness of cyberspace I could be perfect. And even though I'd settled into an apartment and a full-time job, I still felt like a stranger in LA.

The men I met online made me feel like I'd stumbled into a romance novel, where I got to play the sought-after damsel. "You comely wench, ask me on a date and I shall accept," wrote Animal Logic, an arbitrage trader in Chicago. "Let your auburn hair blow in the wind once for me," wrote Ocean Glimmer, a music editor in Greenwich Village. All were charming, but geographically distant.

I felt like King Kong. I could lift up the beige box of my computer and discover a tiny village thriving underneath. When I grew tired of socializing, I could simply return the computer to its original position.

Then one night, I opened an email from Purple Person, which consisted only of a castle built of asterisks. Slowly the castle gate opened to reveal a golden box. In turn, the box opened, and a phone number popped up, in my area code. Finally, a man I could meet without booking a transcontinental flight!

A few nights later, I got the courage to make the call. Purple Person, also known as Zachary, lived in LA's Fairfax neighborhood, twenty minutes north of me. He offered few other details, nor did he ask any of me. There were no questions like "What do you look like?" or "What do you do for a living?" or "How old are you?" I followed suit and asked few questions of him.

After editing all day and chatting on Talk Channel all night, I found myself at a loss for words in Zachary's company. We'd stay on the phone in silence, save for a jazz station playing on his bedside clock radio. I curled up in bed with the telephone receiver cradled in the crook of my neck. It was a relief not having to make small talk; I could just enjoy the pleasure of his company.

During one conversation, a cold breeze blew in the window. For some reason, I asked, "Zachary, what are you doing?"

Without missing a beat, he replied, "Do you feel the chill?"

I was dumbstruck. How could he have known?

"There's a spirit roaming around the city. I'll have to talk to my coven about it. I can't have spirits bugging my friends, can I?"

His voice sounded young. And he was acting like a wizard of some sort, or at least like a guy who dabbled in witchcraft.

In a subsequent call, he said, "I'm confused, Laurie. Your voice sounds like the flow, but your words sound like you're guided by the force."

"What do you mean?"

"The quality of your voice sounds heart-centered, but your words seem like you're all in your head. Maybe you need someone like me to throw the switch, so you can find your way back to the flow."

I'd heard some good come-on lines, but Zachary's was particularly original. I wanted to meet him.

Chapter 10

THE FLOW

"Pay me a visit," Zachary suggested, sending me his street address. He told me he lived with his parents, so I assumed he was way too young for me. Why waste my time? But I was attracted to this perceptive man.

The next day I did a drive-by. His yard was immaculately landscaped, and a capital L in a flourished script decorated the chimney. A late-model Volvo station wagon was parked in the driveway. Zachary obviously lived an upper-middle-class lifestyle.

"When we meet, give me a keepsake," he urged when we spoke the next night on the phone. "Leave me a message on my answering machine. I'll store the cassette, along with printouts of your emails, in my memory box."

What an odd request. I was flattered. Apparently, he expected our association to be worth remembering. At the same time, it hurt to hear that even before we met, he expected our association to end.

After we hung up, I unearthed the heirloom handkerchief that my grandmother "Bumble" had given me. It was blue-gray linen with yellow bumblebees hand-embroidered at each corner. It was worth bestowing to this mystical man.

Then I left a message on his answering machine: "I have something for you. It's old and blue and totally rocks. And, like this message, for your memory box. Come over Saturday afternoon for tea and I'll arrange to give it to thee."

While Zachary wasn't offering a serious relationship, his obvious occult leanings intrigued me. I suspected he might bring much-needed perspective to my stalled romantic life.

For our first meeting, I wore jeans and a cashmere cardigan—form-fitting, but not too tight. I didn't want him to think that this visit was a booty call. At the same time, I wanted to be a woman worthy of a castle built of asterisks. But I still worried that he might be fourteen. After all, Talk Channel did not enforce a minimum age requirement. I'd have to pour him a Coke, pat him on the cheek, and send him home.

When I opened my apartment door, I was pleasantly surprised. He was 6'3", maybe 220 pounds, with long, gently curled auburn hair and pale green eyes behind oval wire-rimmed glasses. I marveled at his open, innocent expression. He looked about eighteen. Attractive then, and I imagined he would grow more so as he matured—his demeanor more self-possessed and his chin more chiseled.

I poured mugs of Earl Grey tea, and we sat on opposite ends of my living room couch. He complimented me on how I'd gotten to know him. "Half the women want to know my measurements and then come over to see for themselves. You get a big gold star for not wanting that."

"Measurements?" I asked. "You mean like your chest size and . . ."

"Yeah, you get the picture."

"Gracious me."

"I like older women. At school, I'm better friends with my teachers than I am with my classmates. In fact, you look a lot like my high school math teacher."

"Gee, thanks." I smiled, then added, "Are you of age?"

"I'm turning twenty in two weeks, if that's what you're asking."

I was relieved he wasn't fourteen and just tall for his age.

After we finished our cups of tea, Zachary said, "Hey, let me give you a quick back rub before I leave."

Uh oh, I thought, *I know where this is going.*

And it did. We kissed for hours on my living room rug. I felt like I'd been holding my breath for months and now suddenly I could exhale.

For the next month, we hung out together. I'd take him along on errands and was always entertained by his company. One day, as we backed out of the grocery store parking lot, two drivers vied for our soon-to-be vacated space. Zachary rolled down the car window and, in a masterful British accent, called out, "I say, milords, do you want our spot? Is that what you're wanting?" We giggled as the drivers glared at us.

After hanging out with Zachary for a few weeks, I no longer woke up with a headache or felt fearful leaving my apartment. My heart slowly thawed.

I considered the men I'd dated since moving to LA. Too often, a Saturday night dinner left me anxious and discombobulated. My dates talked *at* me, not *with* me. They resided solidly in their heads, not their hearts. A low-level depression percolated just below their surfaces. Only by the following Wednesday could I restore my usual level of energy and equanimity.

Eventually, however, I could no longer rally by midweek. My malaise became permanent. I didn't want to admit it, but dating had been sickening me. Zachary was the first man in a long time who energized rather than depleted me.

One afternoon, I picked up Zachary at his junior college. He braced his large bass, which he'd named Dinah, in my back seat. As I drove him home, he sat in sullen silence.

"What's wrong?"

"Does the term 'butthead' mean anything to you?"

"Uh, yeah, although it's not really part of my vocabulary."

"A classmate in the school's recording studio accidentally laid drums over my bass track."

"Oh, Zachary, I'm so sorry," I said, trying not to laugh. I relished his young-man's theatricality.

He consistently tried to lure me to bed, emailing certificates for an *Emergency Massage.* One evening he brought over a VHS tape: *Behind the Green Door*, a porn movie popular at the time. After sitting with him on the couch and watching it for ten minutes, I jumped up and yelled, "This is disgusting. There's no way I can touch you now!"

He stared at me, bewildered that his seduction had backfired.

Hanging out with a twenty-year-old already felt inappropriate, and watching porn together completely unseemly. I harbored no illusions that our relationship would go anywhere. I was, after all, fourteen years older than he was.

Six weeks into our association, Zachary announced, "I'm grounded." His dad had just gotten his BBS bill, dominated by hours of online communication with women.

BBSing was not a cheap hobby. In 1987, online communication cost forty cents a minute. If you lingered online too long, you could rack up quite a bill, like Zachary's recent tab of $350.

"But I can still host visitors," he said eagerly. "Swing by."

I wondered if his "grounding" was a ruse to get me into his bedroom. If he couldn't seduce me at my place, maybe he could try at his.

I drove to the Fairfax district. Is this what my social life had come to? Visiting a grounded twenty-year-old boy? Had I sunk to a new low?

His father answered the door and eyed me suspiciously. Surely, he could see I had no intention of spiriting his son away from junior college and his comfortable Fairfax home. I was simply paying a casual visit to a grounded friend. Dad didn't look convinced.

Zachary ushered me into his bedroom but kept the door open. "Dad's orders," he explained. In the center of his dresser, four flickering votive candles circled a small velvet book. It was wrapped in my grandmother's keepsake bumblebee handkerchief. I drew my fingers across the book's soft cover.

"That's my spell book," he said, scooping it up and sticking it deep in his top drawer.

"Have I invaded the cave of a practicing male witch?"

He laughed.

"Is that a cackle?" I asked, only half in jest. Then I noticed a small dish of water on his bedside table. "What's that for?"

"Oh, that's where mermaids swim," he replied. "I check every morning. None have appeared yet, but they will."

"Really?" I was charmed by his explanation. It could have been that of a wizard or a boy artfully hiding the dish for his retainer. He was the right age for orthodontia.

We stretched out facing each other on his bed. I tried to relax but worried that his father might storm in at any moment to pry us apart.

"I've led six past lives, three evil and three good," Zachary announced. "This one, the seventh, is the tiebreaker."

"Well, you've had a really good effect on me. Ever since I met you last month, my malaise and need to hibernate have miraculously lifted."

I didn't want to come on too strong, lest I scare Zachary away. So I didn't share just how much he contrasted with the more appropriately aged men I'd been dating. He was warm. He was playful. He was heart-centered; my prior male companions in LA were decidedly not. If I was going to thrive, even survive, I'd better pay far more attention to the visceral effect of the company I kept.

"The girl I was seeing before you was seriously sick," he said in a matter-of-fact tone. "It was cancer, I think. But her illness went into remission a few months after meeting me."

"Is that what you do? Am I another ailing woman benefiting from your witchcraft?"

He gave me a Mona Lisa smile.

"I think your seventh lifetime looks promising." I cupped his cheeks between my hands.

As Zachary walked me to the door, he handed me a sealed red envelope.

"What's this?" I said, holding it up to a light to see inside.

He whispered in my ear as he hugged me goodnight, "Don't open it until I tell you to."

Since his father had cut off his BBS account, I could no longer communicate with Zachary as readily. Nor could I visit him with Dad hovering in the background. I felt adrift. I decided to poke around the occult section of The Bodhi Tree, the oldest new age bookstore in LA. Zachary's wizardly leanings had piqued my interest. In an occult encyclopedia, I looked up the definition of a wizard, also known as a male witch. I learned that "the craft of a witch is to alleviate the pain and suffering of fellow human beings, bringing them much-needed solace and succor."

It suddenly dawned on me—I wasn't completely new to the occult realm. Before the advent of cell phones, I had to resort to psychic communication if, say, I needed to change a plan at the last minute. I'd lie on my bed and focus on "call me, call me, call me" when I wanted a boyfriend to phone me on my landline. Amazingly the telepathy worked—on one occasion, even down to the minute.

"Sorry," one boyfriend explained. "I would have called you ten minutes ago when you first contacted me, but I wasn't near a pay phone."

At the time, I hadn't given that ability much thought. I simply viewed it as taking care of business in the most expeditious way. But now that I'd met a likely wizard, I took the ability more seriously.

The men I had met at Great Expectations—the attorneys, the accountants, the optometrists, even the Disney animator—presented a deep rootedness in the material world. I could never venture into topics of a spiritual or occult nature. They would quickly dismiss me. Like most, they lived in the reality of the Third Dimension. Few ventured into the psychic realm of the Fourth Dimension. Hell, most didn't even know it existed.

Zachary, by contrast, could very well have cast a spell on me and maybe even initiated the help of his coven. He'd introduced me to what might very well be the power of the occult. I vowed never again to let a man squelch the seeker in me.

His father couldn't ground him for long. Soon Zachary's answering machine greeting marveled at his new love. "I just wanna tell the world, I've met someone," the greeting began. "And she's beautiful!"

Distraught, I hung up without leaving a message. Even though he was too young to ever be more than a casual friend, I had grown fond of him. He finally called to explain. She was eighteen, the first girl he'd ever dated who was close to his age.

"She's in beauty school and a hair model, too!" And they were sleeping together, he said, something neither I nor the previous woman friend had been willing to do.

I felt enormous jealousy, even though I had no right. And I worried that Zachary's sudden exit might spell the return of my malaise. But I no longer suffered from headaches or nausea. His "cure" seemed to have stuck.

I realized healers aren't necessarily department heads at a university hospital. It might be a Zachary, a twenty-year-old living at home, barely passing music classes at junior college. Similarly, healing is not always of the conventional sort. I might not hop up on a chiropractor's table or chat across a coffee table in a therapist's office. Instead, it might take the form of hanging out with someone whose presence, whether warm and playful or wizardly and psychic, dislodges me from my long-term toxic state. No fancy drugs or ointments. No adjustments or surgeries. All that appeared to be necessary was my openness to Zachary's wizardliness.

Zachary could very well have been a horny teenager on the prowl, not a wizard at all. In the end it didn't matter. He'd pulled me out of my slump and maybe I'd pulled him out of his—for the first time he was dating an age-appropriate woman.

A few weeks later, Zachary emailed an illustration of the red envelope he'd given me. *Open it*, he wrote.

I slipped the envelope out of my lingerie drawer. Inside was a two-by-three-inch photo of him beaming in a red cap and gown. Zachary had my grandmother's bumblebee hankie and I, his Fairfax High graduation picture.

Even though I was almost twice as old as Zachary, in many ways I was much younger. I was oblivious to tools like spell books and covens and to concepts like "the force" and "the flow." But Zachary set that inclination in motion. He whet my appetite to delve deeper into the spiritual realm. Maybe that was the main reason I'd met him.

I never saw Zachary again, but I kept his picture. From time to time, I slipped it out and remembered Purple Person, the castle built of asterisks, and the velvet book with just the right spell.

Chapter 11

JUST FRIENDS

Now that Oscar had nudged me and Zachary had healed me, I was ready to return to the treacherous waters of LA dating and, hopefully, find a life partner.

To improve my chances, I attended a workshop sponsored by *LA Weekly* called "How to Write a Personal." I learned: *Be honest. Be creative. State what you want.* This much I knew already. I dismissed the seminar as a waste of time, until I struck up a conversation with my seat partner, Gigi, a curvaceous Persian woman with a can-do attitude.

She said, "I know just the guy for you. He lives in my complex. Neville's smart, funny, a writer, in his thirties. I think you'd hit it off."

I gave Gigi my phone number, not expecting to hear from him. But a week later, Neville did call. Our conversation immediately fell into an easy rhythm, peppered with his sly humor. It was as if I'd known him my whole life. But right away, I didn't harbor any romantic expectations. I sensed we'd be friends, not lovers.

We agreed to meet at the Novel Café, a converted used bookstore, a few blocks from the beach in Venice. Neville was tall—at least six feet—with long, tanned arms. He wore a utilitarian watch and an odd choice of shirt, which made me like him more—a short-sleeved cotton top printed with floating chess pieces. He hailed from Baltimore. That explained his decidedly un-LA attire.

We struggled to maintain eye contact, to not look down or away as we spoke. We were both shy. But our rapport in person proved just as strong as it had been on the phone.

So many Angelenos, I'd discovered, didn't actually participate in the give-and-take of conversation. They just waited for you to pause so they could begin talking again. Not so with Neville. We were equally curious about what the other had to say.

And with good reason. We had a lot in common. We subscribed to the same magazines—*The Atlantic*, *Vanity Fair*, and *The New Yorker*. We both were Sagittarians. We both meditated. We both played tennis. We both wrote/edited for a living. It was like I'd found my male doppelgänger.

While our conversation flowed freely, we couldn't help but eavesdrop on the couple arguing at the next table.

"You just don't validate me," the man said. "That's the crux of our problem." The woman fell silent, obviously wishing to beat a quick retreat.

Neville and I smiled at each other. "Have you ever said that?" he asked.

"No," I said laughing. "I can honestly say those words have never fallen from my lips."

"Well, the guy may have a point."

"How so?"

"You have to remember all men are dogs," he observed. "You need to feed and shelter them, pet them, and validate them. You know, 'Oh, what a good boy you are today.' Only then will they be happy."

"Interesting. Are you a dog?"

"Yes, Laurie, I'm a dog. But just know," he added, "women, by comparison, are like cats. Pleasing them is much less straightforward."

I was mesmerized by the way Neville's mind worked. I could see I had been right. We would make good friends. I just wished I was also physically attracted to him. But I wasn't. Not at all. Maybe it was his monotone voice. Or just a lack of chemistry.

Neville walked me to my car. But he stood a good eight feet away while we said goodbye, as if I were a bomb about to go off. Was he afraid I might reach over to give him an awkward hug? Maybe he didn't like me at all. But then he asked, "When will we play tennis?" Was that just a polite pleasantry?

Back home, I wondered if I'd ever hear from Neville again. Or if he joined me in my sentiment that we would make far better friends than lovers. I knew how "I'd like to just be friends" could bruise a man's ego, even if he agreed friendship was the way to go.

Amazingly, Neville did call again to arrange a get-together. But quickly I saw our outing was a date. Picking me up, paying for dinner, suggesting that we go back to his apartment to smoke weed. We were not having a friendly meetup. We were having a meal as prelude to getting high and having sex.

I declined his offer to go to his place. As he drove me home, I could feel his dejection. He assumed I had spurned him. I didn't know how to say, "Can't you see how much rapport we share? Let's not throw that away. Let's do what we are meant to be—each other's friend, maybe each other's best friend."

Neville didn't call for a week, two weeks, then three weeks. Finally, I called and left a message. But he didn't return my call. I guess he'd moved on. God knows, there were plenty of fish in the sea.

Then, six months later, Neville called. "What's up?" he asked.

I resisted saying, "You're just *now* getting around to returning my call?" Instead, I matched his breeziness. "Not much. And you?"

Amazingly, we settled into the friendship I'd imagined for us all along. For once, I'd known what I wanted with a man and gotten it.

As we played singles matches, followed by a café au lait, our conversations only got deeper.

"We were born spiritual beings, Laurie," he observed over one coffee. "More so than most. So we have a responsibility, more than most, to develop that capacity."

No one had ever said *that* to me before. "Okay," I gulped.

He suggested we attend a meditation class held at a guru's Beverly Hills apartment. "I hear he's good. The real deal."

"Count me in!" Finally, I was feeling more at home in LA.

Chapter 12

DRIVING LESSONS

At the last minute, Neville bowed out of our plans. "I've got a migraine. But you go. I wanna hear all about it."

I felt uncomfortable going solo. A meditation class led by a self-professed guru in his Beverly Hills apartment? That sounded iffy. But I wanted to prove to my new friend that I was brave and adventurous, that I could be counted on to report back with a funny story or two. I planned to arrive early and enter the guru's quarters only in the company of classmates.

I sat on the front steps of the guru's complex, waiting for other students to arrive. Soon, a white limo pulled up, a chauffeur at the wheel and with what looked like a white wolf (but turned out to be a dog) riding shotgun. In the back seat, a man with gelled hair didn't get out when the chauffeur opened his door. He was absorbed in a conversation on his car phone. A few minutes later a woman in her fifties roared up in a Range Rover with a LIGHTEN UP bumper sticker. Finally, a woman about twenty-two, in a tight tank top, leapt out of an open jeep. I memorized this odd scene to share with Neville.

Feeling safety in numbers, not to mention a chauffeur standing guard at the limo parked outside, I stepped into the guru's tiny apartment.

"Hi, I'm Dr. Deva," a short, pudgy man greeted us. "Come sit down." He spoke with a slight lisp. And his name sounded like "diva."

He wore white silk pantaloons, a string of crystal beads, a gold Rolex, and white patent leather shoes.

The group—about six of us—sat cross-legged on red sequined cushions circling the edge of an Oriental rug. Tiny plumes of smoke rose from incense on a table covered with statues of Indian goddesses.

The woman next to me leaned over and whispered, "Dr. Deva? *Really?*"

I laughed. "With a name like that, he'd better be good."

Dr. Deva began with a short talk. "We create an illusory bubble out of ourselves. Then our bubbles collide with others' bubbles, and everything becomes a bubbly bubble."

I wanted to say, *Hey, buddy, what're ya talkin' about?* But my classmates nodded in agreement. I took notes in a spiral notebook balanced on my knee, hoping one day to pop the bubble of his metaphor.

To mark the end of his talk, Deva hit a gong and instructed us to lie spread-eagled on our backs for a guided meditation. The young woman who'd driven in the open jeep began to cry. The wolf-like dog, restless in the limo, was led to a corner of the apartment, where he panted as he surveyed the room. Outside, the chauffeur argued with someone on his cell phone. Deva rapped on the windowpane and pressed his index finger to his lips.

Despite these distractions, I could feel myself sink into a deep peace. My whole body vibrated. Afterward, I joined the line to hug the teacher. The class emptied as I wrapped my arms around his white-robed shoulders. He held me a long time, then whispered in my ear, "Be still, we're flying away together." Deva's hug and whispered words magnified my altered state. I had to walk around the block several times before I could man the controls of my car.

Much as I grew in my enjoyment of Dr. Deva and the hallucinatory experience of his guided meditations, I couldn't afford to attend regularly. After a month, I explained my finances to him.

"I need to learn how to drive," he said. "How 'bout private meditations in exchange for driving lessons?"

"Wow, sure!"

I picked him up the following Saturday morning. He sported a straw hat with a red ribbon. Instead of his usual white patent leather shoes, he wore brand-new Reeboks. And, through his translucent harem pants, I noticed a yellow undergarment.

"Swim trunks," he explained when he caught me staring. "Students frequently invite me for a Jacuzzi or beach picnic."

Or more? I wondered. I could see I was not the only one attracted to this round man, who was a good three inches shorter than me.

As we navigated the hills overlooking Hollywood, he ground the gears and stalled the car. "So many buttons and levers and pedals to push simultaneously," he lamented.

I considered how much a new transmission might cost.

On Sunset Strip, I pointed out landmarks: Flippers, a disco roller palace; The Comedy Store, where Jay Leno and Robin Williams got their start; and the Whiskey a Go Go, the nightclub that popularized go-go dancing.

"Lean out the window," I told him when we reached the intersection of Sunset and La Cienega. I explained that contestants competing in a contest sponsored by a radio station lived on the three-story billboard above us. "Whoever lasts the longest wins a Ferrari. They've been living up there for months." Several contestants waved as Deva looked up. He shook his head and laughed.

We wound along Sunset Boulevard to Bel Air. At a sharp turn, orange cones narrowed the highway. The driver ahead leaned out his window and tipped over one cone after another.

"I love LA," he said. "You're such children."

And I was beginning to fall in love with Deva. My initial attraction had only grown over time.

Eventually our lessons migrated from the road, to sipping lassis at Bombay Palace, to my apartment in Palms. The yellow swim trunks did, indeed, come in handy. As we kissed on the couch, Deva slipped off my tank top. He drew a mandala in red ink on my right breast—an Om symbol with radiating petals.

"Wait a minute," he said. He pulled some fruit from his satchel. "Now I will give you a mango meditation. Devote all your energy to sucking the juice from the tiny hole in the top," he instructed. "The mango, you know, is shaped like a boob, but it's better because a mango has so much more juice."

He didn't whisper something romantic like "you have pretty eyes." Instead, he observed, "It's hard to find evolved people. At least you're partially evolved."

I winced at his compliment negated by a slight. The obvious implication: he had evolved. I hadn't gotten there yet, and maybe never would.

After he slipped the mango back in his bag, I gently probed about his life.

"Oh, little Laurie, what can I say? I'm intergalactic. The earth is my bed. The sky is my blanket. I'm a man of the universe."

"Have you ever been married?" I asked.

"If I were meant to be a family man, I would have married ten times over. But don't get me wrong, I like women . . . especially women into Kama Sutra. After ten or twelve hours of Tantric sex with me, they experience a high like no other."

I stared at him.

"If you're not into that, I totally understand. Maybe you know some Tantric girls? Someone you could introduce me to?"

I'd noticed that men could take a mercenary approach to sex. "Sex really helps my creativity," one friend noted. "Writing lyrics comes much easier after getting laid." Or "sex gives me a sudden infusion of confidence," explained one paramour. "I feel like the man again!" And here was a third reason: sex as the ultimate spiritual inebriant.

While reasons varied, the result was the same: I got written out of the script. I played only a walk-on part supporting the man's goal, often gleefully stated, as Deva just had, with not a hint of embarrassment. Sex had nothing to do with getting closer to me. Intimacy was of no consideration whatsoever. But I wanted a man as curious to learn about me as I was about him. Not a guy looking for a Disneyland ride.

I stood up. "I've got to get up early for work."

Deva grabbed his satchel with the boob-shaped mango and left without a word.

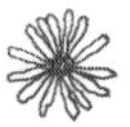

I scrubbed his red drawing off my breast, poured myself a glass of cabernet, and called Neville. "Deva wanted me to be his Tantric sex toy," I told him.

"Well, now there's a stereotype—becoming a guru's erotic slave. So what did you say?"

"I just told him, in so many words, to leave."

"Smart move."

"But the scary part is that, in the past, I might have acquiesced. You know, if I become what he wants, he'll become what I want."

"Yeah, that's an equation that never works."

"So often I've gone into marketing mode," I observed. "Hostess with the Mostest. Erotic Entertainer. Sounding Board. You name it. I could play each role to the hilt."

After a long pause, Neville replied, "That's the problem. You weren't you. You were just playing a role, like an actress in your own life."

"Yeah, I disappeared into my roles. I ceased to exist."

"You became Invisible Girl."

"Exactly."

The next morning, I booked Deva's driving test.

"You think I'm ready?" Deva asked in disbelief.

"Of course," I lied. "It'll be a breeze."

As he pulled away from the curb in my Toyota Corolla, Deva smiled confidently. His examiner, in wraparound shades, stared straight ahead.

Fifteen minutes later, they returned, grim-faced. The examiner said he'd never seen an applicant stall so many times.

"I need more lessons," Deva pleaded. "Pleeeease."

I shook my head. "No, Deva. I'm done."

He may have flunked his test, but I'd passed mine.

Chapter 13

STRANGE BRIDE

I went to bed that night trying to put Dr. Deva as far out of my mind as possible. Chalk it up to a thirty-six-year-old's blind hope: I'd wanted something more with him. But deep down, I'd always known a relationship with a man who called himself Dr. Deva was out of the question. His narcissism would be impossible to live with on a daily basis.

When sleep finally overtook me, another mystery unfolded. I dreamed it was my wedding day. I walked down the aisle unescorted. At the altar, I said my till-death-do-us-part vows.

"You may kiss the bride," the minister instructed.

I turned to my groom only to discover not a man, but a woman in an elaborate lace wedding dress. *How odd*, I thought. *I'm not gay. Why am I marrying a woman?* Nonetheless, I gingerly lifted her veil for the kiss. To my shock, the woman under the veil was me.

The next morning, I called Neville. "What the hell was that about?"

"It's obvious," he said. "The divine, your subconscious, your destiny, whatever you want to call it, is speaking to you in the only way it knows how—with images in your dreams."

"Okaaaaaay. And?"

"Simple. You need to marry yourself."

"Marry myself? How the heck do I do that?"

"Maybe the answer to that question will unfold in time," Neville replied, in his usual calm, steady voice. "Your dream is simply setting the stage, creating your openness to the answer."

"Well, my most recent love interests certainly led me in some other direction than marriage."

"And what direction was that?"

"In a spiritual, not a conjugal, direction."

"Interesting. Well, I'll be curious where the universe takes you next," Neville said, exhaling. I suspected he'd lit up some of the weed he'd offered me on our aborted date. "Be open to the lessons the universe extends to you."

I hung up and considered what I'd just said to Neville. Almost every man I'd met over the past few years had appeared in my life like a carefully crafted character in a fairy tale. As soon as they had delivered a lesson about the spiritual realm, they evaporated. The obscene phone caller taught me about the synergistic betterment I sought in connection, whether the human or divine kind. Purple Person taught me about the healing powers of the occult. Dr. Deva showed me the transcendence of meditation. But I needed to take note. None of these men had stuck around for the romance leading to marriage and children that I sought. Maybe this strange dream explained why. It seemed I needed to look to myself for the support I thought I could only find with a husband in marriage. Was the marriage I sought really with myself?

Chapter 14

CIRCUIT BREAKER

You know how you spot someone, a total stranger, and feel a charge? Could be an attraction or some other reason for knowing them. Well, that's what happened when I noticed a classmate in a candlelit class at Yoga Works.

He ignored the teacher's instructions, stretching into upward dog while others braced in warrior and tilting into inverted triangle while the rest curled in child's pose. His brown hair fell in artful curls. His tank top showed off his toned chest. Despite his strong physique and obvious independence, I sensed a weakened man.

After class, I walked down Main Street to my favorite shop in Santa Monica. I was in the mood for a little retail therapy. As dusk fell and fog rolled in off the Pacific, I spotted the guy who'd caught my attention in class. What a coincidence. I lowered my eyes, too shy to acknowledge him.

"Weren't you in my class tonight?" he asked as I opened the door to the shop.

"Yeah, I think so," I said, trying to sound disinterested.

"I'm going to the Novel Café if you want to join me for coffee. By the way, my name's Brandon." He extended his hand.

"That sounds nice," I replied, surprised by this impromptu invitation from the very guy who'd caught my eye. "I'm going to buy a dress. I'll meet you in fifteen. I'm Laurie." I smiled as I disappeared into the store.

I shuffled through the racks. None of the clothes registered. I tried on a few dresses to kill time.

When I got to the café, I found Brandon sitting at a corner table. He was about 6'2"; his eyes, poignant and blue; his hands, pale and sculpted. His outfit epitomized "Casual Friday"—tight jeans and a button-down, pin-striped shirt.

He told me he was an electrical engineer who'd worked for a local utility after graduating from Michigan State fourteen years earlier. Friends had suggested that I find a nice, stable engineer and settle down. And, secretly, as the daughter of a Cleveland banker who shined his wingtips every morning, I yearned for a stable man like Dad.

Most of my friends, like me, worked in the arts—a far cry from operating a water and power plant. Nonetheless, Brandon and I did share a few things in common: a love of yoga and Midwestern roots.

"You're from Detroit? I'm from Cleveland," I said.

"Yeah, Midwesterners are different, aren't they?" he replied.

As we parted, he asked for my phone number like a man accustomed to getting what he wanted. I wrote it on the back of a grocery receipt, which he slipped in his wallet. We said good night, and I headed to my car, parked up a dark side street. Scared, I looked back to ask him to escort me, but he'd already disappeared into the night.

To my surprise, a week later, he invited me to a chanting session at Yoga Works, followed by a bite to eat.

As I sat cross-legged next to Brandon, the two-hour event seemed interminable. I didn't want to chant with him. I wanted to talk, to laugh, get to know each other, touch.

Afterward, we ducked into a natural food restaurant big on hybrid foods—watermelon/celery juice, blueberry/apple tart, and split pea / sausage soup. In a quiet corner of the hole-in-the-wall, we learned more about each other.

Brandon had chosen electrical engineering to please his electrician father. Besides, he pointed out, "engineering is emotionally neutral. I can just blend in, live in my head, not expose my feelings. It's provided the perfect place to hide. I never have to reveal what's really going on with me."

"I can relate. As a freelance writer, I craft marketing and journalistic copy about everything under the sun, *except* what I feel."

"Guess what?" Brandon said. "I just bought a second car."

This sudden change of subject made me feel unmet, as I so often did on dates. What I had to say seemed like a tennis serve that was never returned. The ball just rolled into the corner. On the other hand, maybe our conversation had gotten too intimate, too soon. Maybe I should respect his boundaries.

"Why do you need two cars?" I asked, taking the bait.

"I *do* like my Camry with its 150,000 miles, but I needed a vehicle with a camper shell."

"To go camping?" I asked, wondering if this was one of his passions.

"No. It's because I have only a few hours of work to do in a day at the Department of Water and Power. I bought a pickup with a camper shell so I can sleep in the parking lot."

"You don't have to stay at your desk? You're allowed to retreat to the back seat of your car?"

"Yeah, management doesn't mind. Everyone does it." He showed no sign of embarrassment. "The parking lot is filled with employees taking cat naps."

Here was a man in the prime of his life. Considering his graduation from his master's program fourteen years earlier, I pegged him at thirty-eight. How could he tolerate such a disengaged workplace? I could see he was hiding out, not just in his profession, but also in his place of employment. His spacey, doe-eyed look, which I'd perceived as deep and mysterious, could very well be the face of a zoned-out, underworked civil servant.

As we dug into our vegetarian lasagnas, I noticed little red bumps creeping up his exquisite square chin. Catching my gaze, he drew his index finger along his cleft.

"The doctors can't figure out what it is," he said. "They're doing tests." He hesitated. "I'm still handsome, though. I'm a good-looking guy, don't you think?"

I nodded, trying not to roll my eyes. No man I'd known had ever commented on his looks so immodestly.

"But, you know, I worry," he continued. "There's this blue vein under my left eye that's getting more prominent as I get older."

"Oh, it isn't noticeable," I assured him. "I see your beautiful smile—that is, when you do . . ."

"I know I don't smile much," he said quietly. "That's because I'm filled with so much sadness. Thank God for antidepressants; they've saved my life. That, and sometimes I just fly someplace where relatives care about me. Within three days my depression lifts."

I began to understand why I'd sensed a weakened man when I spotted him in yoga class.

After our meal, Brandon said, "I really like talking to you. You're an excellent reflective listener. But I don't want to talk anymore."

That was a statement none of my friends ever made. Most were in the "word" business—journalism, media relations, screenwriting—and couldn't *stop* talking. But with Brandon, I suspected silence wouldn't be a problem. I found just being in his company engaging, even consoling. I enjoyed the pleasure of his presence.

"Well, what *do* you want to do?" I asked.

"I really want to kiss your arms."

I was so touched by his sweetness and . . . originality, I invited him back to my apartment for a nightcap.

Brandon used the guest bathroom and noticed the fan was broken. He asked for a screwdriver, and within five minutes he'd fixed it.

"I'm a handyman, too, not just an engineer."

"Oh, to have a handy man . . ." I sighed.

He smiled.

We sat on the couch in the den drinking Coronas. I wanted to learn about the source of his sadness. Before he kissed my arms.

"When I was a baby, my mother took me from doctor to doctor, wondering why I cried so much. Finally, a doctor asked her if she had wanted me. My mother confessed, 'As my marriage fell apart, the last thing I needed was a fourth child.' 'Well, the baby is simply reflecting your sadness,' the doctor told her."

After we finished our beers, he got up to leave. Perhaps, once again, he felt uncomfortable divulging such intimacies so soon. And his wish to kiss my arms had apparently dissipated. Still, he called me a few days later and invited me to drop by his apartment after work on Friday, then play paddleball at the beach.

I didn't want to see his home so soon. I wanted details to unfold slowly. Why skip to chapter 7 when you've barely begun a good book? But I didn't want to hijack the momentum of a budding relationship, so I agreed to the date. I would just avert my eyes as I stepped into his apartment.

The apartment was located in a two-story, horseshoe-shaped complex built in the 1960s and barely maintained, probably due to rent control. His one-bedroom overlooked a swimming pool, too short to swim a good lap and, no doubt, unheated, so no place to linger long. The rubber straps had come loose from the lone chaise lounge on the cement deck, and a barbecue grill for neighborly gatherings had long since rusted.

I wondered if his apartment would be brown, all brown. I suspected it would. Guys like brown. The bedspread, the couch, the shower curtain, even the poor dishes, would be brown. The brilliant blue of the California sky would seep away like a Technicolor movie changing to black and white.

I stepped into his apartment. His furnishings, while not brown, were colorless—an indistinguishable array of beige, gray, and black. A generic oil painting of a sailboat hung above his computer, the kind chained to the wall in a modest hotel. I ran my hand over the plastic Mutual of Omaha topographical map hanging in his kitchenette. He'd probably taken out a sizable life insurance policy to get something like that. On a corkboard, he'd pinned a schedule of swing dance classes and school photos of his nephews. At the top, a round pin read: I AM A RISK TAKER. TODAY I AM GOING TO TAKE A RISK. I suspected it had been handed out at the end of a self-help seminar. His otherwise bare walls and spare furnishings made his apartment look like the digs of a drifter.

"Hey, let's go, while we still have light," he said, pressing his palm on the small of my back and guiding me out the door. As we passed the pool, he grabbed the thermometer bobbing in the water near the ladder.

"What are you doing?"

"You'll see," he said, handing it to me. As his Camry picked up speed, he asked me to hold the thermometer in front of the air conditioner, which was going full blast. "Now hold it out the window against the wind," he instructed.

"Oh, it changes a good fifteen degrees, from sixty-four to eighty," I noted.

"Not bad for a Toyota with 150,000 miles!" he exclaimed. "Now why don't you put it between your thighs?"

"Please, Brandon, I don't think that's necessary."

"Oh, come on," he pleaded.

I put the thermometer between my legs for a second, then checked the mercury. "Oh, my God!" I exclaimed, feigning disbelief.

"What?!" he asked. "What does it say?"

"Off the scale. Hot, very hot."

He laughed. I felt pleased that we'd managed a little flirtation in our usual serious exchange.

But when we made our way from the car to the ocean, he walked a few paces ahead instead of alongside me. I got a chill. One moment he'd pull me close and the next moment he'd push me away.

At the water's edge, we batted a sponge ball back and forth with wooden paddles. I gamely hit it for a good half hour, after which I felt like saying, "Hey, I don't want to volley endlessly. I want to walk along the water's edge and get to know you better." But I figured this game was his way of enjoying the beach with a woman, while still keeping her at an arm's length or two. I said nothing.

Back at his apartment, we ate take-out chicken wraps. Then we retired to the couch. Brandon stretched out. I was surprised when he laid his head in my lap but also pleased. Maybe this relationship was going somewhere after all.

"I feel calm," he said. "Last night I went to dinner at a friend's home. After the meal, I sat with him and his wife at the kitchen table while their two teenage daughters did their homework upstairs. I felt what it was like to be in a house with a family."

Wow, here's a guy who understands the value of home and hearth. I longed to live in a cozy den with my family nearby. Living alone for ten years, I had had plenty of time to burnish that dream. Togetherness seemed not just preferable, but mandatory for my survival.

"I know what you mean," I said.

"Growing up, I never had a role model in any sense—how a guy treats a lady, what a loving family feels like, what it looks like for a man and a woman to be in love."

"Well, it sounds like you're finding role models in your friends, the couple with their two daughters."

Suddenly, he sat bolt upright. I flinched. He pulled up his shirt and displayed his stomach. "I lost two pounds this week. Can you tell?"

With Brandon, every train of thought carried a short shelf life, especially if the conversation veered to anything intimate.

He shook his head. "I worry that I'm going to look like this guy at work—Stan. He's a blob. Pale, never married, with a potbelly that keeps getting bigger. I look at him at the desk across from mine and think, 'Am I going to be Stan in ten years?'"

The phone rang. After he answered, I could hear a woman's voice on the other end.

"I'll call you later. Okay? Okay. Yeah, we'll do something," he assured her.

"Your Saturday night date?" I asked, in no mood to compete for his attention.

"No, just someone I know."

Fifteen minutes later, the phone rang again. This time it sounded like a different woman.

I perused his bookshelf, trying not to listen to the conversation. The shelf was filled with books on how to find and maintain a loving relationship, as well as how to get over a broken heart.

When he got off the phone, I asked, "Your date on Sunday afternoon?"

He ignored my question and led me to the bedroom. As we walked past his closet, I noticed two feet of white button-down shirts hung in a row, followed by pin-striped shirts and an expanse of dark pants.

"I need to maintain a certain image at work," he explained. "Let me show you some pants. I bought eight pairs of $100 pants today."

"That's a lot of pants," I replied. "And they're intended for what? Meet the mayor, get a promotion, go to a barbecue?"

"How 'bout to get me laid?"

"Okay, well, now there's a parameter. I'd suggest starting with a shirt that shows off your biceps." I tried to play along with this banter, but I felt hurt that he treated me more like a guy friend than a date.

"But I don't have biceps. You're the one with biceps."

"Yeah, too much. It's not sexy."

"Oh, I think it is. And I love that small, little curve right there," he added, touching the point where my waist met my hips.

He led me onto his bed and wrapped his arms and legs tightly around me. I was glad I'd worn my new see-through Marilyn Monroe bra and custom-blended rose/musk perfume. Finally, I was making headway. The hell with those other women.

But my efforts at seduction led to nary a kiss or caress. He just held me tight.

The phone rang again. "It's Sylvia. Call me," a woman's voice said on his answering machine. Her tone carried the breeziness of someone he knew well. Brandon gripped me tighter.

After ten minutes in his vise-like grasp, I panicked. I felt more prisoner than paramour.

"So, Brandon, what kind of woman are you looking for?" I asked, hoping consideration of this serious question would loosen his grip.

"Oh, I don't know, maybe a nurse, someone competent like that," he said, relaxing his hold slightly.

Perchance a nursemaid? I felt like asking.

Suddenly, my initial attraction to Brandon made sense. The first time I observed him in yoga class, I saw a cute guy, but also a weakened man. Maybe *that* aspect of him attracted me as much as, if not more than, his looks. He appealed to the first-aid nurse in me. Yes, I knew *that* paradigm well. I do all the listening, assuaging, coddling, and counseling. The men do all the talking, venting, bristling, and complaining. It becomes a downward spiral.

I lay with him a few minutes longer, then untangled myself. "Thanks for the beach and an interesting evening."

"Wait, don't go." He pinned me back on the bed.

"It's a workday tomorrow," I said, squeezing out from under him. "Besides you've got all those calls to return." I grabbed my purse and made a beeline for the door.

Back home, I dialed Neville for his wise perspective. "What's with the Heimlich hold?"

"I think you've found yourself a teddy bear situation."

"He *did* hold me like a little kid clinging to his stuffed animal."

"Teddy girllll!" he sang. "You'll always be my teddy girrllll!"

"Stop it, Neville!"

He laughed and hung up.

The following Thursday night, Brandon called. "We have to figure out how to make money with your voice," he said. "It's so sexy and soothing." He sounded like he knew he had to compensate for all the women who'd called during our date.

"One of the things I admire about you is your ability to nurture and heal," he continued. "I was wondering how we might work on healing together. What form do you think that might take?"

"I don't think so, Brandon. But it was sweet of you to ask." I quickly got off the phone. I was flattered that he perceived me as a healer but also pissed that he didn't view me as anything else.

Boyfriends seemed to want a piece of me, but not the whole of me. Miles wanted me as an accomplice to his Peter Pan. Dr. Deva wanted me as a Tantric sex partner. And now Brandon wanted me as his healer. I felt like a box of chocolates, rifled through for just the nougat-filled ovals. What was up with that?

I grabbed my diary to try to make sense of what had happened.

A therapist once told me, "Intimacy depends on mutuality and availability." A troubled, self-absorbed person, like Brandon, offers neither. With him, I'd become a service provider, tending to his pain. In turn, who I was, what I thought, what I needed, would disappear.

I closed my diary and lay back on my bed trying to fight depression. But then a thought seeped through my malaise. Maybe I should heed Brandon's observation—what he perceived as my ability to nurture and heal. That idea could very well have been Brandon's gift to me. But there was a caveat that he failed to mention: I needed to explore that inclination in a venue other than the LA dating market, where so many lost lambs roamed, ready to rope me into a nonreciprocal liaison. In other words, I needed to explore that inclination in the professional domain.

Chapter 15

LOVE CANDLE

I retreated to my third-floor apartment to regroup. Love for me, I had discovered, wasn't a battlefield so much as a relentless slog. When I lamented to Denise about the sorry state of my romantic affairs, she responded in a surprisingly conventional way: "Finding love is a numbers game."

"By numbers, what do you mean exactly?"

"Two hundred, five hundred, a thousand dates. Whatever it takes."

"I don't know if I have it in me to date five hundred more Brandons, Dr. Devas, or Purple Persons."

I turned to other women friends for guidance. Having exhausted all typical means of "putting themselves out there," several had resorted to magic.

Stacey had written "October 1991" on slips of paper and taped them all over her apartment. "That's the month and year of my wedding," she explained.

And when I visited Elaine, she pointed to a corner of her living room. "Kneel," she ordered. A ten-inch red candle burned on a side table. It was her "cosmic love wish candle, blessed by real monks."

She asked me to pray that love would come into her life. An adjunct religion professor who ricocheted among four community colleges to make ends meet, Elaine craved stability.

I knelt before the flame. "Please, God, bring Elaine a professor," I began in a loud whisper. "Tenure track. Sorry, God, adjunct won't do." I got back up, thinking I'd done my duty.

"Get back on your knees," Elaine commanded.

I knelt again. "One more thing, God, I almost forgot, the man must love dogs, especially Blue. That's Elaine's sixty-five-pound Samoyed."

Amazingly, Elaine's love candle worked. While researching at the Huntington Library in Pasadena, she met a history professor on sabbatical from Indiana State. He was both tenured and a dog lover, as I had requested.

I decided to skip the love candle and reenter therapy. Not with Barbara, but with Joyce, an MSW near me in Palms. Perhaps she could give me some insight on how to manifest a man.

In our first session, she gave me a long penetrating look, estimating whether I could take what she was about to say. "This is outside my area of expertise," she began, "but have you ever thought about making your hair more poofy?"

"You think it's too . . ."

"Yes, too flat, especially on the sides."

I ran my fingers through my chin-length bob to give it more body.

"Let's be honest, Laurie. Men are very visual creatures."

Still cringing at my diagnosis, I walked home from my appointment. I remembered the first question my mother asked the doctor when she delivered me: "Does she have curly or straight hair?" When the doctor said it was definitely straight, Mom let out a sigh of relief. I had not inherited the wild curly hair she hated so much. Now, it was painfully evident: I needed my mother's hair, not my father's fine, pin-straight locks.

At the corner, I passed a CVS. Hell, let's solve this problem right now. I invested $39 in twelve super jumbo hot rollers with bonus clips. The package promised "voluminous curls" and "high-powered shine." Maybe the solution to my problems was simpler than I realized. Maybe it all boiled down to something as simple as poof.

Eventually, though, I discovered poof contributed little to my search for a man.

Quickly engaged and wishing to spread her wealth, Elaine bought me my very own love candle for Christmas. I slid the tall red pillar, wrapped in gold tissue paper, deep beneath my bed, like a grenade that had to be kept still lest it detonate.

Finally, as December 31 approached and it came time for New Year's resolutions, I carefully unwrapped the gift and set it on my altar, next to my collection of seashells and the elephant god Ganesh. I lit the candle and smelled its intense jasmine and sandalwood scent. I tried to pray with the identical intent that I had marshaled in front of Elaine's cosmic love candle, but I could not muster the same level of focus. My goal was not as clear-cut as a tenure-track professor who loved my dog. I wanted something, to be sure. What it was, though, I did not know.

On New Year's Eve, I lit three votive candles on my nightstand and climbed into my tall brass bed. I found my diary buried under the down comforter and propped it on my lap. Time was growing short. The new year was minutes away. I needed to come up with an alternative to Elaine's love candle, some other way to manifest what I wanted. I wrote:

Why rely on God? Or happenstance? Or a stupid therapist? Why not write your ideal romance? Make it happen, girl. I know you can! You can fill it with intrigue and uncertainty, all the while knowing the story ends with your happily ever after.

Chapter 16

BLIND DATE

The next day while chatting on Talk Channel, I came up with the beginning of my romance novel.

I'd been corresponding with Blue Moon for a good month, both online and "voicing" over the phone. But we couldn't bring ourselves to take the next logical step—meet in the flesh. He was afraid I'd find his nose too big. I was afraid I wouldn't look like his type.

"Maybe we should meet in total darkness," I joked.

"Wow, a true blind date! Let's do it!" Blue Moon said to my surprise.

So, just like that, I created the plot of my first scene, as well as cast my costar—Blue Moon, also known as Sebastian. Perfect!

Next, I stepped into the role of set designer and visited my local fabric shop. Covering my head like a Halloween ghost, I tested bolts of cloth against the glare of the window. A clerk led me to a densely woven white cloth. "Makes a room pitch-black at high noon," he said. "All the Holiday Inns use it."

That night, I did a darkness check. I taped the blackout fabric to the picture window in my living room and stuffed rags under my front door. As my eyes adjusted, I unplugged every source of light. I unstrapped my sports watch with its glow-in-the-dark dial. I masking-taped the electric red numbers on my cable box. I unscrewed the lightbulb in my refrigerator. I stepped back and surveyed my handiwork. I'd achieved total darkness. My apartment, covered with colorful David Hockney posters and usually flooded with sunlight, had become a darkened den and, hopefully, not the scene of my murder.

"I'm in your lobby," Sebastian whispered in my intercom. He was right on time—8 p.m., a good hour after the sun had set.

"Take the elevator to the third floor," I directed. "Go to Apartment 302."

I cracked open my door, then hid as far from the incoming hall light as possible. I kept my glasses on even though it was pitch-black. I practiced reaching for the chain on my floor lamp in case the darkness grew too scary.

"Laurie?" Sebastian called out as he opened the door an arm's length without stepping over the threshold.

I was so nervous my saliva had dried up. I drew my tongue across the top of my mouth to wet it. "Yes," I whispered. "It's me."

I could hear Sebastian edging closer. It was too late now to back out of our outrageous scheme. I was glad I'd at least taken some precautions. We'd exchanged copies of our driver's licenses with the photos cut out. When I received his copy, I studied his birthdate in February, remembering that I had dated an inordinate number of Aquarius men. He was the age stated in his Talk

Channel bio—forty, a year younger than me—and his address in Santa Ana also matched the city he'd listed in his bio. Still, I imagined an LA prosecutor entering the document into evidence prior to Sebastian's murder trial.

I mailed a Xeroxed copy of Sebastian's driver's license to Neville, with *I trust you will avenge my death* penned across the top. When Neville got the missive, he left a message on my answering machine: "Oh, my God, Laurie. Dating in LA has finally gotten to you. You've gone mad!"

"Where are you?" Sebastian asked, slowly sliding along the hallway wall. His voice filled the room—three-dimensional compared with the way it sounded over the phone and heightened because I could see absolutely nothing.

"Can you believe we're really doing this?" I whispered.

He didn't answer. He was focused on navigating a strange room in the dark. As he reached the end of the hall, he paused. "Ninety-degree turn," I called out.

He inched closer and found me on the couch. He sat down, but only for a few seconds. "Let's stand," he said. Guiding me in front of him, we slowly made our way from behind the coffee table to the corner of the living room. "You can go first," he said.

I touched the skin on his forehead. It was smooth and moist with sweat. I drew my fingers farther down to the nose in question. It was large, but nicely sculpted. As I lightly grazed his lips, I could feel him smiling. His tie felt like silk, tied in a double Windsor knot. I squeezed the knot and said, "I can tell what kind of a guy you are." Then I pulled away. I didn't want our encounter to become sexual.

"No, keep going," he said.

Through his shirt I felt the texture of his chest hair. "Brown?"

"That's right," he said with a chuckle. I remembered that he had written in his bio "My hair is gray, but the hair on my chest is brown."

As I moved farther down, I brushed his thighs. They were large and hard.

"I bike a lot," he explained.

Last, I felt his shoes. They were heavy, laced, with tiny perforations in the leather. I flashed back to my father's wingtips.

"So how do I feel?" he asked.

"Substantial. Like I've never known how substantial a human being is."

"Okay, well, I'll take that as a compliment. Now it's my turn."

Sebastian began with my head. "Your hair feels blonde."

My heart sank. *Is he going to be disappointed that I'm not a blonde bombshell?* "I'm a brunette, remember? It's just fine like a blonde's."

"Your face is so small."

No one had ever said that, but it was true. I often had to buy children's glasses.

Next, he lightly touched my breasts. "Nice," he said, then squeezed my waist, signaling that he was going no further. "Now, why don't you take me on a tour of your apartment?"

I took his hand. It was large and warm. I led him to the jewelry box on my bedroom dresser. Since we shared a penchant for old-fashioned jewelry, I poured my favorite charm bracelet in his palm. Next, I guided his hand to the four-armed brass elephant on my altar.

"I can't imagine what it is."

"It's Ganesh," I whispered, "the elephant god who removes all obstacles."

"Good, I'm glad He's here tonight."

It was such a relief to talk without a phone pressed to my ear and to touch his hand. We sat on the floor. Sebastian rustled what sounded like paper in his pocket. "Open wide," he said.

"I trust you'll put something good in it."

He found my mouth and slipped in a homemade butter cookie covered in powdered sugar. Accentuated by the complete absence of sight, the flavor exploded in my mouth.

"I stole it from my godmother's wake." Sebastian lived an hour south in Santa Ana, so he'd planned our first date to coincide with his trip to LA for the Friday night memorial.

"I'm sorry I never got to meet her."

"She was pissed that I left her wake early. But now that she's met you, she understands why."

"She's here?"

"Yes, I can feel her with us."

I tried to imagine the ghost of his godmother joining us as we fed each other butter cookies. We kissed. But I pulled away after a few seconds.

"What's wrong?"

"It feels strange kissing a man I've never seen."

"I could solve that problem right now. I felt the wall switch when I came in."

"No. I want the night to be pure, totally dark."

"Okay," he said. Then after a long silence, he added, "Well, maybe it's best that I get going."

I guided him to the living room wall. "Just go straight ahead and you'll find the door."

We gave each other an awkward hug. I could hear him slowly slide along the wall, then struggle with the door handle. I hid in the darkest corner of the living room so I wouldn't see him, and he wouldn't see me when the light from the hallway flooded in.

"Bye, Sebastian."

"Shall I say, 'I'll look forward to seeing you soon?'"

"How 'bout *being* with you again?" I called out from the corner.

He laughed. "Bye, Laurie. It's been a pleasure."

The door latched behind him, and I could hear the bell of the elevator door. I sat on the couch where I'd begun the evening. The room sounded loud in the dark. It took awhile for it to fall silent again. I drew my fingers along my face and breasts, imagining how they felt to Sebastian. I reached up and pulled the chain of the floor lamp, squinting as my eyes adjusted.

The room looked like a stage set. The brown paper bag holding the butter cookies lay crumpled in the middle of the living room carpet. Masking tape crisscrossed the blackout fabric stretched across the sliding glass door to my balcony. Pictures on the wall hung askew. That's where Sebastian had slid.

In the morning, I found an email from Sebastian: "I was so disoriented after I left, I had no idea which way to drive. I've been thinking about you all day. We were so brave. It made me feel we could be brave in other ways."

Chapter 17

LET THERE BE LIGHT

The next morning, before I'd even gotten up, Neville called. "You're alive! I don't need to avenge your death! For the love of God, why can't you meet a date for coffee like the rest of us?"

"I've been on too many coffee dates."

"But there's judicious risk-taking and then there's downright danger, girl." Neville's voice was uncharacteristically insistent.

"I can read people. Sebastian is safe."

"Famous last words," Neville said, hanging up in exasperation.

On the phone that night, Sebastian and I agreed we needed to have our first "light" date and soon.

"Just think," he said, "we haven't really met yet. We haven't shopped for skates or waxed the car. Maybe next time we meet, we should go bowling."

"Bowling? But a bowling alley is so loud and fluorescent."

"Exactly."

My heart sunk. I wasn't ready for bowling, at least not yet. The bright lights of a bowling alley represented exposure, judgment, and potential rejection. Maybe we wouldn't like the way the other looked. I preferred the more forgiving darkness of our initial encounter. Thankfully, we decided to meet in the dark one more time.

As I taped the fabric once again across my picture window, I discovered the afternoon sun was harder to block out than the streetlights at night. Maybe we'd have to settle for dimness rather than darkness. We agreed that after one hour we would light a candle in the next room, then every fifteen minutes bring it closer. That way we could slowly materialize before each other's eyes.

This time Sebastian knew the drill. When he opened the door, he called out a cheerful, "It's me!" and slid along my hallway wall with more assurance than the first time.

"I'm closing my eyes till you get here," I said. "I'm sitting in the middle of the living room."

We sat cross-legged, facing each other. "Welcome to our second date," I said.

"Do you think 'dating' is really the right term? I mean, isn't dating like going out to eat and seeing a movie?"

As we sat together, I noticed sounds that I'd ignored in the light. My neighbor, a magician, kept doves on his balcony; they were cooing. Church bells rang for afternoon mass. Sebastian and I sat listening, breathing, our toes touching.

At the appointed time, I lit the first candle on a hallway table. As my eyes adjusted, I could just make out Sebastian's profile, nothing more. He had a large square face and a glint in his hair, which had turned gray at age fifteen. "Nerves," he'd explained.

"Sometimes I feel like you're licking my brain," he whispered.

I was used to that kind of remark from Sebastian. But now I had the added challenge of sewing his odd observation onto the dark silhouette before me.

We lay on the carpet and hugged. He was wearing what felt like a sweatshirt, not the silk tie and dress shirt of our first meeting. I pulled his cuff. "Gray, black, brown?" I asked.

"Turquoise."

I'm hugging a man in a turquoise sweatshirt, I told myself. I tried to settle into the arms of this man wearing a turquoise sweatshirt.

"It feels so good to be silent with you for a while," Sebastian said. "That's the problem with the phone. You have to keep talking."

I tried to enjoy the silence, too. But our long, deep breaths were too distracting. Then a loud rip jerked us apart. The sun had unglued the masking tape holding up the blackout fabric across the picture window. We ran to the hallway to hide, but it was too late. As the afternoon sun flooded my apartment, I buried my face in his shoulder.

Then I slowly pulled away. Sebastian was classically good-looking, with olive skin, a Roman nose, and deep-set chocolate brown eyes. But he didn't hold himself with the confidence of a handsome man. And while he'd prepared me for gray hair, his salt-and-pepper curls surprised me. They made him look older than his forty years.

I held his head in profile. With his strong features, he looked like an ancient landowner. But I couldn't paste his looks—old-world patriarch—onto his actions: meeting a stranger in total darkness.

He squeezed my hand. "I thought you were going to be just cute with your small face, but you're beautiful."

I hoped he wasn't just being polite.

"Let's go bowling," he whispered in my ear.

"Alright," I said meekly.

"Just testing you," he said, with a laugh. "You're off the hook. A client booked a last-minute appointment this afternoon." On his online profile, Sebastian had listed his occupation as "relocation consultant," whatever that was. Our dates, or should I say "encounters," were so otherworldly, a practical question such as "What exactly do you do for a living?" never got asked.

Offering to walk him to his car, I locked my apartment door. We pushed the button on the wall and waited side by side for the elevator to come. He didn't look at me and I didn't look at him. We just stared straight ahead, like the two strangers that we were, weathering the awkwardness of waiting for an interminable elevator. Finally, unable to stand the unanswered question—*So what do we actually think of each other in the light?*—I punched open the door to the stairwell and descended the steps two at a time.

"Hey, what's the rush?" Sebastian called out, galloping behind me.

When he unlocked the door to his car, a weathered Saab, I saw a rubber pretzel on the dash. "Oh, do you have a dog?"

"No," he said. "When I get stuck in traffic, I chew on it instead of grinding my teeth."

I slipped it in his mouth. He gnawed on it like a frolicsome puppy.

"LA traffic'll do it to you," I said. Sebastian's creative way of dealing with LA's gridlock made me like him all the more. As he pulled away, I waved, relieved that we'd finally met face-to-face.

That evening, Sebastian invited me on a proper date—to chow mein the following Saturday at his apartment, one hour south in Santa Ana.

"Oh, my God, your first light date!" Neville marveled later. "I can hardly wait to hear what happens next. But give me his address, just in case."

I walked into Sebastian's ground-floor studio apartment, just a few paces from his Saab. His entire apartment was strewn with boxes. A Panasonic stereo container served as his bedside table. Boxes stacked in the kitchen cabinets had been carefully marked: Lightbulbs, Utensils, Glasses. His only unpacked possession—an Apple computer—sat on a Bekins moving box.

"Did you just move in?"

"Been here almost two and a half years," he said. "I like to feel like I'm always ready to move. I never want to feel like *this* is it."

I tried to convince myself Sebastian was simply charmingly quirky, not a madman. But I wondered whether I should run for it while I had the chance.

Taking me on a "tour" of the apartment, he motioned to the blank walls. "It's so much more compelling than paintings or photographs. I can imagine what I want to be there." *Interesting*, I thought, *both of us share a penchant for what* could *be, not what* is.

He served me coffee in a sugar bowl because his mugs were packed. We ordered take-out chow mein and ate in the middle of his Oriental rug. As I sat cross-legged, trying to navigate chopsticks, he opened up about his life over the past year.

He had proposed to his girlfriend of ten years—a bank teller with hair down to her waist. A month before the wedding, she sent him a letter saying she'd never loved him.

"How awful. What did you do?"

"I stopped eating for two weeks. Then I picked myself up and tried to date again. I asked women sitting alone at the movies if I might join them. I attended gallery openings, but everyone came as a couple. Finally, I went online and became Blue Moon."

His handle suddenly made sense. He *was* blue when he joined the dating site.

We ignored the king-size bed three feet from us and sat farther apart than we had in the dark. I quickly finished my chow mein and stood up. "It's getting late. I have an hour drive." I said goodnight, then drove in silence back to Los Angeles. As I sped up the dark 405, with few billboards or defining landmarks, I felt like Sebastian's dislocation had rubbed off on me.

I stopped to call Neville from a gas station pay phone, unwilling to wait until I got back to LA. "I've attracted yet another lost, depressed man. He's a relocation consultant who appears incapable of relocating himself."

"What the hell is a relocation consultant?" Neville asked. "That sounds like a made-up title."

Sebastian emailed me the next day, no doubt from the Apple computer perched on the Bekins box: "I'm looking five hundred miles down the road. I see clear skies. We're going to wind up together."

Heartened by his optimism, I gave the relationship a chance. We drove back and forth between LA and Santa Ana every weekend for six months—playing tennis (in the dark, of course), flashing the cops on the roof when police helicopters whirled overhead, and once in a while, doing something normal like sharing a beer and catching a Wimbledon match on TV.

Eventually, we had sex. But I was sorry we did. One night, I noticed his mouth as he entered me. It was a horizontal line one moment, then pulled into a smile like a kid on a carnival ride. He wasn't in love with me, I could see that, but he wanted to be. Just as I wanted to be in love with him. We searched each other's face waiting for it to happen.

But the better we got to know each other, the more silent Sebastian grew. He'd just take a deep drag on one of his many Marlboro cigarettes and say nothing.

Finally, I admitted defeat. My screenplay had not yielded a happily ever after. Once again, in my journal I tried to make sense of what had happened with Blue Moon.

I really outdid myself this time. Instead of veering into a simple role, something easy like first-aid nurse, I went a step further: I orchestrated an entire Hollywood production. And what, in God's name, for?! It made me feel powerful, in control, desired—all things I rarely feel in my normal dating life. But an even sadder truth, one that's harder to admit—I had come to believe no one will ever love me as is, for the pure, unadulterated me. I had to add set decoration, a screenplay, and the adrenaline rush of danger. Even then the man might not fall in love with me. The solution? Oh, something easy like, say, learn to love myself, develop faith that there is someone out there who likes me as is, right out of the box. Or maybe, just maybe, look elsewhere for love, somewhere beyond the romantic arena.

I staged the breakup scene at Van Gogh's Ear, a coffeehouse in Venice.

"As fellow performance artists," I began, having memorized my lines, "we were a perfect match. We set up happenings, like in the sixties—blackout nights, tennis in the dark, flashing police helicopters. But other than that, we didn't connect—not intellectually, not sexually, not spiritually. No wonder we never fell in love."

Sebastian was his usual silent self. I suspect he agreed with my assessment, although I couldn't be sure. After a minute of looking down, swirling the foam on top of his coffee, he turned red and blurted, "Take a good look at this face, 'cause you're never going to see it again." Then he stormed out of the café.

Immediately, I felt enormous relief. The ruse had come to a blessed end. Still in screenwriter mode, though, I wanted to rewrite his parting line. It seemed trite, not in keeping with our unconventional liaison.

Later, in a little online sleuthing, I discovered Sebastian was actually an Orange County real estate agent. In my diary that night, I wrote:

A depressed, chain-smoking, low-performing realtor appeared far more appealing when he billed himself as "Blue Moon" and a "relocation consultant." But then, look at me, I could hardly talk. I had preferred to meet in the dead of darkness rather than in the light of day. I had wanted to hide who I was, too. Why? I'd never felt fully seen and enjoyed. I'd always felt sidelined, never the main attraction. I had to write an enticing role for myself to earn top billing.

Chapter 18

ASKEW

After I broke up with Sebastian, I decided to move. Gang warfare had migrated to my tiny community of Palms. Every night, gunshots rang out and police helicopter searchlights swirled around my bedroom.

When I inherited a little money, my family urged me to buy a condo. "You gotta get on the real estate escalator," they advised, "before you're priced out of even a starter home in LA."

I hired Zelda. "The Jewish grandmother you never had," my mother called her. Every week I hopped in Zelda's bottle-green Jaguar to tour every condo that came on the market. We bounced over the potholes of West LA, like a motorboat jumping waves on the open sea.

How exciting, I thought, *to buy my first home.* But as we toured properties in Brentwood, Santa Monica, Mar Vista, and Playa del Rey, I got an uneasy feeling.

The heart-shaped Jacuzzis, the massive master bedrooms with cathedral ceilings, and the tiny third-floor lofts perfect for a crib were designed for a couple with children. To make matters worse, the real estate agent hosting the open house often asked, "Would your husband like a tour, too?" I preferred my unremarkable 650-square-foot one-bedroom, perfect for an occupancy of one.

Six months and 150 condos later, Zelda wanted to fire me. She doubted I would ever make a decision. Then she showed me a three-bedroom, three-story townhouse in Santa Monica, within walking distance of the beach. Built in the mid-1970s, its amenities were more modest—bathrooms with only one sink; lower ceilings; and a tiny third-floor bedroom, perfect for a playpen but also for a home office.

Zelda was relieved. So was I. But my relief was short-lived. I balked at the mountain of escrow papers I had to sign and at the words typed under each signature line—"Laurie Collister, A Single Woman." Moving felt out of the question. I couldn't bear to dismantle my bookshelves, take down my Hockney and Rothko posters, and strip the balcony of its potted plants. A relationship might blow up, a boss might yell at me, but I could always retreat to my third-floor sanctuary.

Not until the movers called to say they were two hours away did I consider boxing up my belongings. Eventually, with only minutes to spare before the van pulled up, my mother, brother, and I stuffed clothes, dishes, and books willy-nilly into plastic drawstring bags.

"Wow, getting you moved is like scraping moss off a rock," my brother observed.

Mom and Peter had always lived with a spouse, a girlfriend, or a dog or two. I envied their companionship. They had what I had wanted and, seemingly, had gotten it effortlessly. My Palms apartment, absent that company, had become almost like my partner. And now I was getting a divorce.

As I feared, the excess space in my new home felt like a constant rebuke. I was living in a home designed for three or four residents, not one.

At my apartment, my neighbors were mostly singles. If they had company, it was a boyfriend or girlfriend who spent the weekend before leaving Sunday night. Now my neighbors in the other nine condos were couples with children, grandchildren, cats and dogs. By comparison, my unit felt eerily empty and silent. When I returned home from evening yoga, I turned on every clock radio, boom box, CD player, and TV I owned to give the impression that my new home was bustling with family.

And I made sure I planned an activity every evening, be it a phone conversation with a friend, a rented documentary, or a hot bubble bath. If I failed to keep myself properly occupied, to give myself "company," I couldn't fall asleep the whole night. Awake at 3 a.m. one night, I realized loneliness had become my full-time job.

Absent a mate, I turned to other ways to connect—with God, through meditation and prayer, and with myself, through journaling. A rigorous morning routine of both practices kept my isolation at bay. The minute I woke up, I sat up in bed, propped my back with pillows, slipped a yoga bolster under my knees, and set a timer for thirty minutes. I shut my eyes, cleared my mind, and focused on a point at the center of my forehead.

Initially, I listened to "When You Wish Upon a Star" on a small audiocassette player. Even as the tape wore out and the lyrics grew distorted, I continued to listen. When the tape broke, I meditated in silence for the first time. To my surprise, my training wheels were no longer necessary. In fact, the silence deepened my meditation. Each day I felt 1 percent more calm, more grounded, more confident than I had the previous day.

After meditation, I knelt at my grandmother's hope chest, covered with seashells, Ganesh, a photo of an Indian guru , and six votive candles flickering in the gloom. I always began the same way, reciting the first two lines of a twelve-step prayer: "God, I offer myself to Thee—to build with me and to do with me as Thou wilt. Relieve me of the bondage of self that I might better do Thy will."

Last, I climbed into a chair behind my great-great-grandmother's secretary and wrote in my diary, at least six pages but longer if I had more to say, and usually I did. I was never at a loss for words.

These two hours were immensely soothing. In addition to providing a sense of connection, meditation and journaling fulfilled my craving for mystery, revelation, and coherence—elements often lacking in my everyday social interactions. Yet I continued to question devoting so much of my morning to these pursuits. My therapist, Joyce, called my meditations "numbing out," someplace where I hid from rather than embraced my feelings. Besides, shouldn't I be getting ready for work? Shouldn't I be at the gym getting my body in shape? But when I skipped that two-hour regime and began my day without it, I felt unmoored. Everything looked like a Salvador Dali painting—distorted and askew.

Chapter 19

MANHUNT

Spring pressed against my window. Even blocked by blackout curtains, the bright rays of April seeped in. New birds joined the chorus in the ginkgo tree that brushed against the pane.

Why not take my meditation outside? I laced up my tennis shoes and headed out the door. At first, I walked slowly on my street—Sycamore—with my eyes closed, until I stumbled over a stretch of sidewalk lifted by tree roots. I opened my eyes but made a concerted effort to keep my mind as empty as I always did in my sitting meditation. I took in the sights. Fuchsia bougainvillea spilled over a gate. Four-story-high palms swayed in the wind. Seagulls glided against a turquoise sky. I tried to become what I saw. I didn't look at the bougainvillea, I became their pink. I didn't look at the birds, I flew with them.

After twenty minutes, when Sycamore hit San Vicente, I turned around, now filled with the same calm ecstasy I experienced during my seated meditations. The forty-minute walk made a perfect addition to my morning spiritual practice.

The next day, though, I took a different approach—to survey my new neighborhood, like a tourist setting foot in an exotic land.

Entire blocks had been destroyed by the 1994 Northridge earthquake the year before. That's how I'd gotten my condo dirt cheap. The owner—a civil engineer—considered his home doomed goods. He moved his wife and young son two thousand miles away, leaving me to my bargain digs perched on the edge of the San Andreas fault. I laughed at the sign posted in front of one flattened apartment complex: UNDER RETROFIT.

Outside the post office, a crumbling Venus de Milo statue held a bouquet of yellowing broccoli. A man sat cross-legged as a pet white mouse scampered across his shoulders. I dropped a dollar bill in his can and asked the mouse's name. "Destiny," he said. The homeless in Santa Monica, I could see, were more erudite than most.

Hankering for a snack, I popped into Wild Oats and surveyed the baked goods in a glass case. Tucked between the chocolate croissants and blueberry muffins, I spotted my favorite cookie—a gingerbread man with currant eyes and a smile of chocolate icing. As I reached in to grab one, I read the sign. It was not a gingerbread man; it was a gingerbread person.

Munching on my politically correct cookie, I headed west on Montana to the beach. Inching down the steep driveway of Yoga Works, a patron navigated her SUV with a giant cup of coffee and cigarette in one hand. Further down Montana, a subcompact's bumper sticker—MY OTHER CAR IS A SALAD—heartened me.

At the beach, I stood on a windy promenade overlooking a wide beach and the ocean beyond. Near the water's edge, a man threw a fluorescent orange boomerang. It glided a hundred yards, U-turned, then flew back into his hand stretched high above his head.

"Santa Monica is a place you can wrap your arms around," my real estate agent, Zelda, had promised. Hoping to live out that description, I signed up for an Artist's Way workshop, sponsored by the city's recreation center. At the first session, we had to chat with a partner, then share what kind of animal we'd like to be. Michael, a fifty-something Brit who worked as an archivist at a maritime museum, said, "I'd like to be an owl. That way I can turn my head 360 degrees and always be predator, never prey."

I tried not to be distracted by Michael's lilting accent and his thick black hair pulled into a ponytail.

"And you?" he asked.

"I'd like to be a poodle. That way I can count on regular shampoos, cuts, and cuddles."

"Yes, their pom-poms are adorable."

Was he flirting with me? Before I could answer that question, the teacher asked us to move to the next person.

In another exercise, we had to write our mission statement. I read mine to Michael: "I tap my talent to listen, intuit and communicate so as to facilitate an individual's personal growth."

"Nice, very nice." Michael extended his left hand to give me the more intimate "Hollywood" handshake.

The exercises were kind of embarrassing, but if that's what it took to get to know my neighbors in Santa Monica, so be it.

I bought a twenty-class series at Yoga Works—one of the first franchises to turn yoga into a cult-like activity. At a candlelit prana yoga class in Venice, the teacher, Steve, straddled my legs to adjust my downward dog pose. I could feel his penis, loose underneath his yoga pants, plop onto the middle of my back.

Hey, yogi Steve, did you forget to wear your underpants? I wanted to ask. But before I could, he leaned over and whispered, "I'm offering a partner yoga class on February 12." He pointed to a ravishing brunette a few rows over. "Danielle is co-teaching it with me."

Ninety percent of the students were women, some A-list celebrities with their entourage in tow, some artfully tattooed hippie chicks with a record deal. Few men—save a husband, boyfriend, or lone twenty-something—showed up. I needed to look elsewhere for my plus-one.

In my six-month cruise of condos, more than one real estate agent had referred to "Magic Starbucks," at the corner of Montana and 7th Street. "Whatever you want—a romance, movie deal, or reconciliation—you can find it at Magic Starbucks," they promised. I chalked up this assertion to real-estate hype but wanted to check it out for myself. Maybe the coffee shop, with its wraparound patio and proximity to the beach, was a spiritual vortex of some sort, like the caves of Sedona.

After making the ten-minute walk from my condo, I bought a cappuccino, then wedged myself between two men deep in conversation and a woman buried in a book. It was the cult classic *Creative Visualization*. I felt too shy to ask what she hoped to materialize, but maybe the universe was giving me a sign that I needed to read the book, too.

On the other side of me, two men talked about giving up cigarettes. "Oh, I tried to quit," one said, "but I began to feel all these emotions—intense nostalgia, for instance—so I stopped trying to quit."

"Yeah," his friend replied. "Feeling is vastly overrated."

Here was my cue to join in if I dared. "Hey, I couldn't help but overhear your conversation," I began.

"You trying to quit, too?" one asked.

"Well, in a way. I've noticed colds and flus are like smoking. They give me a vacation from having to feel. It's gotten so I welcome the interlude."

They didn't quite make the connection—that smoking and sniffles served the same purpose, a welcome numbness in an increasingly jarring world.

I quickly excused myself. "Nice talking to you," I said, getting up to leave.

As I walked home, I cringed at my attempt to insinuate myself in a conversation that was obviously private, perhaps between lovers. Maybe I needed to take a more direct approach in my attempt to "wrap my arms" around Santa Monica.

While Great Expectations had not yielded any romantic prospects, maybe placing a personal ad in the local hip newspaper would prove more fruitful. If I crafted the copy just so, I might attract not only a mate but also a compatriot to join me on my ongoing spiritual journey.

The next day, I placed an ad in the *LA Weekly*:

OPEN HEART and mind. Writer, 5'8", 133,
brn/grn, Midwest roots, seeks SM 35–48 into the arts,
psychology, and a faith. Call Box 4925.

Men left messages like this one: "Hi, I'm Noah. I'm 6'2", 190 pounds and what can I say? I look like the Marlboro Man. I own six rottweilers and a burro that I say hello to every morning. I'm looking for a woman who'll join me on my farm an hour north of LA, a woman who'll say hello to my burro, too."

A second suitor, a retired equestrian from Ireland, upon reading *Primal Scream* had moved to LA to enroll in the Primal Institute. "But I'm having second thoughts about becoming a Primal Scream therapist," he said in his message. "Once the anger comes out, it's hard to keep a lid on the biscuit tin."

"You're a weirdo magnet," Neville observed.

"But in my ad, I talk about my Midwest roots and desire to meet a man with a faith. How odd is that?"

"Girl, weirdos can smell you a mile away."

My therapist, Joyce, urged me to go out with Noah.

"You mean, audition for a role on *Little House on the Prairie*?"

"Why not? Doesn't every gal want to go out with the 'Marlboro Man'?"

Eventually, I scheduled an early dinner with a man named Sam, who wrote a 1980s cult film with "vampire" in the title. My brother looked him up on his professional IMDb account and recited all the TV shows and films my date had worked on. "He's legit," Peter promised. My brother loved participating vicariously in my manhunt. Working in the film biz, models, production assistants, and actresses practically fell in his lap. He never had to explore venues like Talk Channel, Great Expectations, or the *LA Weekly* to meet his next girlfriend.

I arrived at the 17th Street Café in a flowered cotton dress I'd just bought at the Gap. Sam looked like a guy who wrote about vampires—his hair so black it probably was dyed, and dressed in all black when that look was more funereal than hip. Somehow, we got on to the subject of elementary school. He shared his experience at a Catholic school in New York City, how hard it was to cut out a snowman with scissors designed for a right-handed child when he was left-handed. The nun mocked the ragged edges of his paper snowman.

Our exchange felt more like a therapy session than a first date. As I struggled to make conversation, it became apparent that I knew more about Sam than he'd revealed in his sixty-second *LA Weekly* voice message.

"You vetted me, didn't you?" he hissed.

My face said it all.

"How could you?"

Continuing a date with a pissed-off man who wrote about vampires felt unwise. "Let's call it a night," I said, getting up to leave before the first course arrived.

"On, no, we're gonna finish this dinner, young lady."

As I inhaled deeply to calm down, the third button of my bodice popped open. He could have made a joke about my wardrobe malfunction, but he did not.

Even though I'd lost my appetite, I plowed through my meal. At least I could show some decorum even if my vetting had not. After dinner, I wanted to disappear into the night, to walk the five blocks home, but Sam insisted on driving me in his boat of a Chrysler sedan.

He idled in the middle of Sycamore as I scrambled out of the car. "Thank you for the interesting evening," I managed.

"Yeah" was all he said before he hit the accelerator and tore down the street and out of my life.

When I got home, I found a phone message from Michael, my classmate at the rec center. We had exchanged business cards after a recent Artist's Way class. Would I join him for a picnic lunch on his boat? Talk about good timing. I called him right back.

Watercress and butter sandwiches with the crusts cut off felt so British. And Michael had brought a chilled bottle of white wine to wash it down. We started to make out before we opened my contribution: a box of gingerbread people.

He pulled away. "Laurie, I have something I need to tell you. You know Dee in class?"

I recalled the tall, buxom blonde with pin-straight bangs and large hoop earrings. Instinctively, I'd known she was competition, referring to her as "Double-D Dee" in my diary. "Yes," I said quietly.

"Well, we live together. We have for the past five years. But it's a practical thing. We're more like roommates now."

"You mean roommates who sleep together?"

"Yes," he said, "but only occasionally."

I remembered Michael's desire to be an owl, a creature who is predator, not prey. In this instance, I felt decidedly like the prey, and not like my favorite animal—a cherished poodle. Now I understood why he'd arranged our picnic in the hull of his boat. It was well hidden from public view.

Sidelined yet again. With Dr. Deva, it was by Tantric sex. With Brandon, it was by his persistent sadness. And now, with Michael, it was by Double-D Dee. Launching a third-party romance, I'd learned, was never a good idea.

"I like you, Michael, but I'm not about to duke it out with Dee." I grabbed my box of gingerbread people and ran for shore.

Chapter 20

CHATEAU SYCAMORE

A few months after moving into my condo, I found a letter slipped in the crack of my door. Susan in Unit #6 was holding a meeting the following Sunday. The letterhead, in a swirly purple script, read *Chateau Sycamore Homeowners Association.* At the bottom of the page, Susan had handwritten "We look forward to getting to know our new neighbor!"

Part of the allure of living in a condominium complex was the chance to join a close-knit community. I loved dorm life in college. Wasn't condo dwelling simply the adult version?

If there was ever a time to make a good impression, this meeting was it. I devoted an hour to getting ready. I rolled my pageboy in my new electric curlers, polished my nails in frosted silver, slipped on a herringbone skirt and a pair of high heels. I walked ten paces to Unit #6, wobbling in the pumps I rarely wore.

"You came!" Susan exclaimed when she opened the door. "I'm so glad you did." She escorted me to her sunken living room. "Hey, everyone, this is Laurie, our new neighbor in Unit 4."

I smiled and nodded at people I might live next door to for years, if not decades. The women wore leggings and rhinestone flip-flops that showed off immaculate pedicures. The men, all in monochromatic colors, wore jeans and ball caps. They stared at my outfit, suitable for a Fortune 500 board meeting, not a casual evening get-together.

I tried to make light of our contrasting attire. "I figured I better dress up for a meeting of the Château Sycamore."

They laughed politely. One man called out, "Hey, we didn't name it. Some idiot before us came up with that."

I slunk to an armchair in the back of the room. Susan called the meeting to order. "As you know, this is election time. We need to nominate new officers."

She handed out ballots, along with a list of the seventeen homeowners. I stared at the sheet. I was on the list, even though my escrow had closed only a few months earlier. "It will be anonymous," Susan announced. "Take out your pens, vote, fold into quarters, and return to me."

Since I didn't know anyone on the list except for Susan, I felt at a loss about how to vote. I chose the owner of #5 for president, a petite brunette who'd smiled at me as I lugged a tall ficus on moving day. I eenie-meenie-minie-mo'ed the other two positions.

Susan collected the ballots and retreated to the kitchen to tally the votes. In her absence, my neighbors peppered me with questions: "Where did you move from?" "What do you do?" "Do you have children?" My former residence in Palms (decidedly middle-class), my profession (media relations and freelance writing), and my number of children (none) perplexed them. They couldn't peg me.

Susan returned with the election results. Loretta in #7, who turned out to be a CPA, had won the natural role of treasurer. The petite brunette in #5 had been chosen as vice president. "And, drum roll, please," Susan announced, drawing out each syllable. "Our new neighbor, Laurie, has been nominated president!"

My mouth dropped open. Momentarily speechless, I finally sputtered, "Shouldn't I become a member of the association before I lead it?"

"No, the job is simple," the neighbors said in chorus. "You'll take to it like a duck to water. Besides, of all of us here, you actually *look* like a president."

"I'll sleep on it," I said, before I tottered home on my heels and fell face-first on my bed. Then I got the bright idea of ringing Zelda. She'd know what to do.

"I am clueless when it comes to home repair. I know nothing about management. And the one time I did my own taxes, the IRS audited me. What am I going to do?"

Zelda offered these words of wisdom: "Accept the job. It means you can upgrade your home—be it landscaping, the roof, the tile, what have you—to your own tastes. It puts you in the driver's seat of your biggest investment."

Then I called Loretta, the new treasurer. "I've got you covered with the books," she insisted. "You'll know where every penny goes."

The next morning, I called Susan. "I've decided to accept the position." I paused. "I'm honored."

"I'm so glad. It'll give us all a chance to know each other better."

Susan was right. We *would* get to know each other better. From the outside looking in, my neighbors seemed like model citizens—a divorced school principal and her adopted daughter; an attorney and his stay-at-home wife; an architect, her husband, and their cute two-year-old son. But at our monthly HOA meetings, I saw an entirely different side. Husbands interrupted and sometimes slighted their wives' comments. And two units didn't pay their monthly HOA dues. When I mentioned the legal consequences of lapsed payments, without naming names, one of the culprits shouted, "How dare you!"

The shortfall in dues quickly became a problem. Mysterious leaks in the garage led to the discovery that the building's foundation needed resealing. A specialist met with me to describe the procedure, known as "flashing." But his explanation was so uninteresting and his eyes so mesmerizing, all I could concentrate on was one question: *Are your eyes blue or green or a perfect combination of the two?*

Resealing the foundation proved small potatoes compared to what came next. Restaurant Row on nearby Montana Avenue, a booming business in the 1990s, burst a sewer line. The collapse broke our complex's pipes, flooding the garage with three feet of sewage. I called State Farm and the Santa Monica manager of sewage to explain the situation, using as calm a voice as I could muster. But I lost it when I called a friend: "I'm knee-deep in shit!"

Heavy rains called for a new roof and an infestation of termites meant a five-day evacuation and a $25,000 tented fumigation.

"We're working our way through every scourge in the Bible," I lamented to Loretta.

"Yeah, and paying for it, too," she observed. Each repair required tens of thousands of dollars in homeowner assessments, on top of the monthly $500 dues.

That night, in my journal I wrote: *The very things society told me would yield the greatest pleasure—home ownership and romance—are the very things that have proven the most burdensome and disappointing. What's up with that?*

A few weeks later, I drove to my old apartment in Palms and parked on the palm-lined street near the entrance. I noted that the new tenants had attached a window box of pink geraniums to my former balcony. I looked longingly at my old third-floor bedroom. How often I'd gazed out that window at the tops of the three palms. When the toilet clogged or the ceiling fan stopped, I called the on-site property manager, who quickly handled the repairs. I managed 650 square feet, not a ten-unit complex with seventeen often contentious homeowners. I called Neville from my car to wax longingly about my previous home.

"Are you stalking your old apartment?" he asked.

"That would be a yes," I said. I lingered a few minutes more, then slowly drove away.

Chapter 21

A YOGI MOVES IN

After a few years in Santa Monica, I finally found the perfect place to worship. The church held its Sunday services in a tiny chapel on the banks of a man-made stream overlooking Altadena. The international Hindu organization, founded in 1912 by an Indian guru, didn't just talk *about* God, as many denominations did; it taught members how to directly experience the calm and ecstasy of God's presence. Considering how tumultuous condo politics had grown, I needed that experience now more than ever.

One Sunday, as I walked from my car to the 11 a.m. service, my stride fell in line with a fellow parishioner. Francisco and I knew each other by sight, but we'd never spoken. He introduced himself and handed me his card. YOGA TEACHER / MASSAGE THERAPIST / MEDITATION COACH, it read. I smiled at the hybrid.

"Come to my yoga class," he urged.

"Okay, why not. Sounds fun."

"I hold them in the community room of my apartment complex in Marina del Rey," he said. "It's next Saturday at 5 p.m. The address is on the card."

I looked forward to the experience—a class outside the corporate chain of yoga studios. Especially intriguing, Francisco looked kind of like a guru—high cheekbones; flawless light-brown skin; slight, enigmatic smile; and small, round wire-rimmed glasses.

The following Saturday, I poked my head inside the designated community room. Francisco sat in the lotus position with his eyes closed in front of a room bereft of students. I cleared my throat to get his attention. He slowly opened his eyes.

"Are the other students coming soon?" I asked.

"They all canceled," he said.

"So, I'm the only student?"

"Looks that way."

"Do you still want to hold class?"

"Definitely."

For a moment, I wondered if there *had* been other students. Maybe "let's do yoga" had become the new "come over to see my etchings" line. A little self-conscious, I gamely followed his routine of sun salutation, warrior pose, inverted triangle, and shavasana. After ninety minutes, the colors in the room shimmered and my persistent stress slipped away.

After class, Francisco invited me for tea at the apartment he shared with a roommate. The red bulb in his desk lamp cast a warm glow over his tiny bedroom. In the dim light, I could just make out the outline of a massage table leaning against the wall and a black cat sitting on the back of an armchair.

"She's my roommate's," he said. "Say hi, Polka Dot."

The cat studied me, motionless, except for her tail, which was slowly waving. Easy-listening jazz played in the background.

When I placed my tea on a paperback book, Francisco gently slid the mug off the face of a guru on the cover.

"Whoops, sorry," I said, swiping the moisture away with the back of my hand.

Francisco smiled and leaned in to kiss me. The purple paisley bandanna wrapped around his head slipped off, exposing a broad swath of bald head. He'd collected the black hair growing along the sides into a ponytail. Sporting his ubiquitous scarf, he looked like he had a full head of hair.

Within ten seconds, Francisco had stripped down to his yellow-and-white striped bikini briefs. He reminded me of an exotic dancer who disrobes with a single pull of a drawstring. He managed to remove my top and bra just as swiftly.

"Hey, not so fast!" I said, pulling my clothes back on.

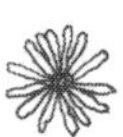

Still, each week I returned for his private yoga class followed by a dip in the pool, tea, and a little kissing under Polka Dot's unwavering gaze. He never ripped my clothes off again.

One time, as I luxuriated in the post-high of yoga and evening swim, Francisco said, "I'm moving out," as quietly and casually as if he'd said, "I need to pick up a carton of milk."

"What for? You've got it great here—the pool, Polka Dot, a room for teaching yoga."

"I just can't make the rent."

"Where will you go?"

"I have nowhere to go," he said, falling silent. "I guess I'll have to live in my car."

"Don't be silly," I said without thinking. "You can live with me till you get back on your feet."

"Really?" he said, brushing my cheek with the back of his hand. "You'd do that for me?"

"Of course. My God, we can't have you homeless."

"Wow, thank you so much. You're such a good friend."

As I drove home, I regretted my decision, but it was too late to rescind the offer. *It'll be fun*, I tried to convince myself. *I could use the company.*

The following Monday night when I got home from work, Francisco was waiting at the curb, his Honda Civic packed to the roof with all his worldly possessions.

I showed him the couch, which folded out into a bed in my tiny guest room. "It's surprisingly comfortable," I assured him.

He nodded, but he was more concerned about his altar. "Can I set it up on the coffee table in your living room?"

"Be my guest," I said. "It could use something better than takeout containers and *Newsweek*."

He carefully stretched out a purple embroidered cloth and covered it with photos of gurus, a wooden incense burner, two votive candles, and a bronze statue of Ganesh.

"May Ganesh bless us," I said, patting His head. "I have an elephant god of my own on my bedroom altar."

Francisco leaned his massage table in the corner of the living room. I agreed he could see clients at my condo while I was at work, hoping he might save up enough money to move out.

Within an hour of his settling in, I cranked open my ironing board, a rare occurrence, and started ironing items I usually left rumpled—placemats, pillowcases, even my dish towels. I put fresh linens on the pull-out bed, making hospital corners, no less. Never had a man brought out my domestic side. None had made me want to "nest."

When I stumbled out of bed the next morning to make coffee, in the corner of the living room, Francisco stood on his head. He waved his arms in circles. Short bursts of breath pushed his stomach in and out, like a bug performing a mating ritual. Living with a yogi, I could see, would be exotic.

On the way home from work the next day, I bought a bouquet of pink lilies. Then I popped into the gift shop above the Hare Krishna Temple and picked out a tiny orange dress with shimmery gold borders. During holidays, Hindu devotees festoon their altars. I wanted to do the same for Francisco's altar to mark the occasion of his moving in.

At home, I arranged the flowers throughout the house and, when Francisco wasn't looking, slipped the dress I'd just bought on the elephant god—not an easy feat, considering its four arms.

While Francisco brought out my long-buried domestic side, I did not bring out his. Instead of using the cutting board, he sliced cheese directly on the kitchen counter, leaving tiny marks. Nor did he rinse his dirty dishes and put them in the dishwasher.

"Does loading the dishwasher threaten your masculinity?"

"Well, I've never had a dishwasher before. I'm afraid I might catch my male organ in the door."

I laughed, forgetting my pique. He was often funny. And when I laughed at his jokes, the sound sprang from a place deep within me. Even more startling, his presence enlivened me in a way I'd never experienced before.

"What are you doing to me?" I asked.

"It's my hot Latin blood."

I smiled. "That must be it."

But since he'd moved in, we hadn't even kissed. Living with me wasn't a prelude to a deepening romance. He needed a place to stay, and I had one. Simple as that. I suspected that my newfound enlivenment had less to do with his sex appeal and more to do with his spirituality. I reaped the benefits of his daily yoga and meditation like a contact high. Whenever he meditated, I felt like I'd just drunk a glass of champagne. Communion with God, I discovered, does double duty. It affects not only your own self, but also everyone around you.

What didn't feel good was the fact that we shared almost no common interests. No, he didn't want to see *American Dream*, the latest documentary about unionized meatpacking workers. No, he didn't want to catch the David Hockney retrospect at a local museum. I'd turn on my favorite TV show, *Unsolved Mysteries*. "Come on, don't you want to solve this week's mystery?" I'd ask Francisco. He'd shake his head and leave the room.

But we did share one thing—a passion for all matters spiritual. Over the next month, we got up at 3:30 on Tuesday mornings and drove in silence to a predawn kundalini class led by white-turbaned teachers in a candlelit Sikh temple. We studied the *Bhagavad Gita* at a Friday evening workshop in our church's chapel. And when a ninety-four-year-old Russian yogi came to town, we quickly bought tickets to her lecture.

We fell into a comfortable routine. While I was at work—now at a nonprofit downtown—he presumably saw his massage clients. Then one evening, about four months into his stay, the doorbell rang at 7 p.m. I squinted through the peephole. A pretty blonde woman stood at the front door.

I looked over at Francisco and whispered, "Do you know who this is?"

"That's my massage client," he said, taking his dinner plate to the sink.

"I thought we agreed you'd see clients just during the day when I was gone."

"She was only available in the evening," he said without apology.

I answered the door.

"Hi, I'm Star Dust," she said, extending her hand.

Francisco greeted her at the door with a warm hug and led her into the living room. I stood at the edge of the room watching. With a loud clang, he unfolded his massage table. Star Dust pulled off her blouse and silk cargo pants, then lay face up on the table, stark naked. Her body was just as stunning as her face.

"Well, I'd best leave you two alone," I said, retreating to my bedroom.

I sat on the edge of my bed trying to digest what had happened. I realized how vulnerable my possessions were to Francisco's parade of clientele. Strangers like Star Dust might have sticky fingers. And I really didn't know my housemate *that* well.

Thankfully, there was one saving grace to Francisco's stay. Instead of watching *The Today Show* with my morning coffee, I'd gotten in the habit of meditating with him as he posed cross-legged at his altar.

One morning, just before I closed my eyes to meditate, I caught sight of a photo, wedged between the gurus on his makeshift altar. It was a faded black-and-white snapshot of Francisco and his family. He was about five years old, at the wheel of a boat. What looked like his father stood behind him, holding his shoulders. The people on either side appeared to be his mother and sister. "Disneyland" was written in a loopy script across the top.

"You look like you had a nice childhood," I commented.

"Well, it sure wasn't a Disney movie."

"What do you mean?"

"My father was an alcoholic. He'd come home drunk. My parents' yelling would wake my sister and me."

"I'm so sorry."

"My mother, in her second unhappy marriage, would take out her frustrations on me, criticize me, yell at me, hit me. I felt so out of control."

"Do you still talk to her?"

"No, she and my sister died in a car accident while visiting family in Mexico."

"I'm so sorry, Francisco."

He went on to explain that his massage practice was a way to gain the mothering he'd missed out on in childhood. "To nurture is to be nurtured," he explained.

"But what about girlfriends?" I asked. "They can nurture you, too."

"I've been so hurt by women, I can't afford to expose my emotions anymore. That's why religion is so good. In meditation, I can feel free to love and be loved by God, but without the pain that comes with romance."

I hadn't gotten there yet, but I could feel myself moving in Francisco's direction. Meditation, at least up to that point in my life, had delivered far more solace, far more of the flow of love he spoke of, than any romance ever had.

My irritation about his four-month stay melted into sympathy and a yearning to heal him. Until a few weeks later, when I found a $10 bill on my kitchen counter.

"What's this?"

"Oh, that's to help with the mortgage."

"To help with the $2,500 mortgage?"

"That's right," he replied, without a trace of embarrassment or irony.

I realized Francisco might need a place to stay indefinitely. That wasn't going to work, especially since, in two weeks, I had to take a business trip. I felt uncomfortable leaving him and his clientele alone for ten days in my home. To make matters worse, Francisco had once confided that to make extra money, he offered clients a happy ending. I could just imagine the headline: *HOA Prez Ran Secret Seaside Brothel.*

In my desperation, I came up with a plan. That evening after work, I swung by the ATM. I withdrew thirty crisp $20 bills. Back home, I sat at the dining room table with a glass of wine and the pile of twenties, waiting for Francisco to return. I couldn't concentrate on TV or a book. I sat in silence, my face hot with anticipation.

Eventually Francisco stepped in the door.

"Have a seat," I told him. "We need to talk."

"We do?"

"You need to leave when I go away on business."

"You don't want me to live in my car, do you?"

I slid the $600 toward him. "Here, this money should tide you over. I checked with the YMCA. You can rent a bunk there for $18 a night. I've reserved a bed for you already."

"Oh, come on, Laurie. Don't be like that."

Maybe it would be okay if he stayed at my place in my absence. But maybe it wouldn't. I didn't back down. I just looked at him firmly.

"Okay, okay, I'll move out."

We avoided each other for the next two weeks. I felt so guilty and anxious. Was I being selfish? But when his exit date came, he packed like he had all the time in the world. He even brushed his teeth. With his backpack slung over his shoulder, he paused at the door. "I'll return for the rest of my belongings tomorrow evening," he said with a businesslike formality.

I nodded without looking at him.

He put his copy of the condo key on the kitchen counter and slipped out the door without saying another word.

I lay on my living room couch and studied Francisco's altar, still intact on my coffee table. Even though we had shared few common interests and not even much conversation in our six months of living together, his company had dramatically affected me. A testament to his daily spiritual practice, his presence automatically put me in an altered state—calm but energized. By contrast, men of a less spiritual nature—that is, the majority of them—decidedly did *not* do that for me.

I remembered catching sight of Francisco that first morning, standing on his head in front of his newly set up altar. I realized my initial impression of an exotic bug performing a mating dance was right. He *was* mating . . . with God. Francisco had exchanged earthly romance for divine love. Maybe I should, too.

Chapter 22

HALLUCINATIONS

After the tumult of Francisco's exit, I tried to return to life as normal. But during errands around Santa Monica, something strange started to happen. At the post office, the grocery store, and the dry cleaner, I heard unexplained sounds. Exiting the post office, metal hit metal. As I parked at the grocery store, brakes screeched. While hanging my clean sweaters on a back seat hook, glass shattered.

"Am I hallucinating?" I asked Neville. "Could I be schizophrenic?"

"I think it's your stress level," he assured me. "Harboring a difficult housemate took a toll. I'm sure those sounds will pass once you settle in and feel more at home in your life."

Bead shopping in downtown LA's jewelry district turned into just the kind of relaxing Saturday I needed, until I came to Ocean and 14th in Santa Monica. My mind still mentally poring through bead trays, I took a left turn into oncoming traffic.

After the SUV hit me, every car in the busy intersection stopped as if in suspended animation. The SUV driver poked her head through my shattered windshield. When I appeared okay, she screamed, "What were you thinking? You could have killed us both!" In shock, I couldn't say anything.

As I climbed into the front seat of the tow truck, the driver said, "Ma'am, it's totaled."

I twisted to gaze through his dusty back window. My Toyota dangled at a forty-five-degree angle, the passenger side crushed beyond recognition. The vision brought back the sound effects I'd heard for weeks. Had some force tried to warn me? If so, why hadn't I listened?

That evening my brother Peter and I had planned to meet for dinner and a psychic fair. "We can do it another time," he suggested when I told him about the accident. But I rarely saw my baby brother. Not even a near-fatal collision could change my plans.

Still shaken, I sat on a steel folding chair facing my psychic. I wasn't there for great wisdom, just intriguing entertainment.

"I see you suddenly pushed to the left," she began. I nodded. "And I see someone really angry at you."

"Wow, she was good," Peter marveled later. His psychic reading was nowhere near as accurate.

Later that night, I studied my psychic's credentials on her business card. She had graduated from a psychic institute in Santa Monica. On the school's website, I learned that a civil engineer turned clairvoyant had founded the institute in 1995 to teach students how to discover their psychic abilities. If my reading was any indication, the school delivered on its promise.

Perhaps my hallucinations had been psychic premonitions. Earlier in the year, I'd dismissed a persistent dread until a garage attendant pointed to a nail stuck in my front tire. And, in the past, when my beau at the time dated a woman on the sly, I woke up in the middle of the night, experiencing their date. Psychic college could help me understand these inklings. The next day I signed up for the institute's introductory class.

Chapter 23

PSYCHIC COLLEGE

The psychic institute bore no resemblance to Harry Potter's Hogwarts school—the dark, scary castle on the banks of Black Lake. Instead, it consisted of two fluorescently lit classrooms, rented off hours from a secondary school in Santa Monica's commercial district. But the minute I walked in, the rooms felt magical—exceptionally calm, centered, and ebullient.

"You've just entered psychic kindergarten," the teacher announced to the seven students seated in a semicircle in the classroom. As she collected empty chairs and stacked them in the corner, she explained, "We wouldn't want any vagrant spirits joining us tonight." I tried to suspend my skepticism.

The teacher, a woman named Carmella in her forties with a thick mane of brown curls, continued, "We live in a vortex of energy and experience energy exchanges all day long. Some people 'throw' energy at everyone around them. Needy people often vampirize others' energy supplies. This school teaches techniques for moving energy to achieve what you want."

I flinched as the classroom door sprung open. People paraded in, wearing fuzzy bedroom slippers. "This is the Healing II class from next door," Carmella announced. "They're here to practice their techniques on you."

A freckle-faced man in his early twenties, sporting chartreuse fur footwear, introduced himself to me. "I'm Bradley. I'm going to be your healer tonight." He pulled my chair to a corner of the room. "First, I'll feel your aura. It's the energy field roughly three feet around your body. It reflects everything that's going on in your life."

He began to circle me, waving his hands as if conducting an orchestra. I clung to my purse for protection. He gently lifted it from my lap and placed it on the floor. "We don't heal purses," he said. "That's in the advanced class."

I chuckled while Bradley burst into gales of giggles. As he circled me, he loudly yawned and belched. Sensing my concern, he leaned in and whispered, "You have a nice aura—light, fluffy, and smooth." I suspected this comment was a common pleasantry in the psychic realm.

"Now I'm going to release energy that's not yours so you can reclaim your own."

Bradley circled his hands two feet from my body, as if waxing a car. After ten minutes he said goodbye. Grudgingly, I admitted to myself that my loud, seemingly rude healer had affected me. I felt lighter, calmer, even see-through.

Then, just as quickly as they'd entered, the Healing II students departed.

"So how do you feel?" Carmella asked.

"Free! Excited!" my classmates and I exclaimed.

"But why did they constantly burp and yawn and laugh?" I asked.

"Those are techniques for releasing energy," Carmella explained. "Amusement, especially, is like psychic Drano. It allows you to get rid of heavy, stuck energy, like invalidation, uncertainty, and judgment. Basically, healing is about finding stuck energy, letting it go, then reclaiming your own."

"And the bedroom slippers?" a classmate wanted to know.

"Oh, it was 'Fuzzy Slipper Night.' That's yet another way to keep the energy in the room light and moving. In this workshop, you'll learn how to be healers, too, not just of yourself and others, but of all aspects of your life."

Wow, I could sure use that knowledge, especially when it came to healing the pain of my aloneness. But Carmella's promise seemed too good to be true.

I returned home to a voice message from the homeowner in Unit #9. He'd found a nest of termites in his closet. I yearned to return to the effervescence of the psychic realm. Instead of responding to my neighbor's call, I looked up the word "psychic" in the dictionary. It meant "relating to the human soul." Based on that definition, a psychic institute sounded like exactly where I needed to be right now. I'd deal with the termites, but carnal matters, at least during this six-week class, would take a back seat to my study of the soul.

In the second class, Carmella spoke about what had led her to psychic college. Sensitive to energy, she found it impossible to perform even the simplest task. Grocery shopping, she often abandoned her cart mid-aisle. All the energy she soaked up became overwhelming. "We are taught that energy doesn't exist. Yet we live in a vortex of energy bombarding us in all directions. At the institute, I learned tools for not taking on others' energy. I'll be teaching you some of those techniques tonight."

Sitting bolt upright in blue plastic chairs designed for grade schoolers, my classmates and I learned to run an imaginary cord from the base of our spine to the center of the earth. Through this "grounding cord" we poured all the energy that wasn't ours. I shrunk Joan, a former toxic boss, and sucked her down my cord. Next, we gathered our own errant energy in a golden sun above our head and let it stream down our spine.

Carmella asked us to conduct one healing before the next class. "It can be anything," she said. "Your husband, your car, your dog, whatever."

I returned home, dubious that I could achieve what freckle-faced Bradley had accomplished with me in our ten-minute healing. But before I retired every night, I dutifully sat on the edge of my bed, my bare feet planted on my avocado shag carpet, to run a grounding cord and build a golden sun.

The next week students shared their homework. Simon, a thirty-two-year-old casting director, healed his sharks. When he cleaned their tank, instead of jumping out the way they usually did, they lay quietly at the bottom. Lisa, a Malibu yoga instructor, healed her house, filled with her husband's World War I memorabilia collection. "I've been living with the ghosts of dead soldiers," she explained. "But after healing my house a few times, it's like fifty windows flew open. It even smells different."

"What about you, Laurie?" Carmella asked. "How did your healing go?"

"Well, I can't claim such dramatic results," I began. "But now I don't wake up with my usual three-aspirin headache."

"That *is* dramatic!" Carmella exclaimed.

"It is!" my classmates chimed in.

"Sometimes you'll discover you were carrying a five-pound sack," Carmella told us. "And then you'll ask yourself why the heck you didn't toss it aside a long time ago."

Exactly, I thought. I shuttered to think how much emotional baggage I needed to throw overboard.

By the fourth class, we were ready to manifest what we wanted in our newly cleansed space—what Carmella called a "mock-up." But first, we had to measure our "havingness," what we felt we deserved. Carmella guided us in our meditation. "Picture a gauge with a needle that can move from 1 to 100. Move the needle to the highest number possible."

One classmate possessed such high havingness, the needle shot past 100. Another classmate's score couldn't make it to 5. I achieved room temperature, about 70.

"Now picture what you'd like to create," Carmella continued. "Include specifics. Drain everyone's energy out of it. Put that image in a clear rose and release it to the universe."

Carmella regaled us with her successful mock-ups: a fruit basket when she was home sick, a handmade necklace from a friend, even a Mercedes. "But you have to start small," she warned. "A small success will give you the confidence to mock up something bigger."

Over the next week, I heeded Carmella's advice—start small. I mocked up a single, gleaming penny. All week, I scoured the street, store aisles, bedcovers, everywhere I frequented. But I never found a coin. While Carmella could manifest a luxury car, I couldn't conjure a single shilling. Maybe I needed to work on my havingness. At week's end, however, as I retrieved a pen from my brother's kitchen floor, I spotted a penny lodged under his dishwasher. Green with age, not gleaming, the coin at least approximated my mock-up.

"I found the penny!" I cried. I held it high above my head and danced in a circle. "I finally did it!"

Peter stared at me, concerned about my sanity. I explained my homework assignment.

"Well, you might want to shoot a little higher," he said wryly. "Maybe a nickel next time."

My brother was right. I needed to aim higher. Nothing in my life worked. Not romance. Not where I lived. And since the crash, not even my car. I needed to change all aspects of my existence—a tall order, but glaringly necessary.

But could I? Should I? Wasn't I lucky to live in a townhouse a fifteen-minute walk from the beach? And I'd always learned something new from every man I dated. Wasn't that success of sorts?

I listened to an audiocassette Carmella had recorded for us. She outlined all the techniques she'd taught to date: grounding cord, golden sun, havingness meter, mock-up, and—my favorite—putting others' negativity in a rose and releasing it. I vowed to practice the five techniques twice a day for one month, then assess their worth.

The next morning, I performed my mock-ups for the day. I wanted a management consultant to sign a six-month retainer for my writing services. I wanted a plane flight to go smoothly. I wanted an editor at *Whole Life Times* to accept my story. I set each mock-up in a see-through rose, then watched it float up and disappear into the clouds.

I found little support for this new endeavor. My evangelical friends feared I was "dancing with the devil." Work colleagues considered "all that psychic stuff" a sign of a midlife crisis. Neville dubbed it "magical thinking." I was choosing some alternative reality that none of my loved ones wanted to share with me or even discuss.

In spite of the naysayers, I pressed on. Amazingly, some of my mock-ups came true. Not just the penny discovered under Peter's dishwasher, but the contract with the consultant, the story placement in *Whole Life Times*, and the flight to visit my father in Cleveland. When the ticket agent told me all the seats had been taken, he switched my reservation to business class on another flight. He even gave me a round-trip ticket as compensation for the change.

True, not all mock-ups manifested. My application to RAND, a think tank in Santa Monica, never made it past HR. And I never found a friend at psychic college. Still, my other successes emboldened me to perform the riskiest, but most imperative mock-up of all—a friendly HOA meeting.

Thirty minutes before the meeting started, I sat on my living room couch and took three deep breaths. I grounded the room. I envisioned the homeowner who frequently shouted and another who often stormed out. I shrank each and sucked them down the grounding cord to the center of the earth. For sound effects, I recalled the satisfying whoosh when my dental hygienist sucked water with a tiny hose from my mouth. I mocked up a meeting with jokes, friendly banter, and respectful listening.

After the meeting, the treasurer Loretta whispered in my ear, "Tonight, everyone was so much more, how shall I say, well behaved." We watched HOA members laughing as they trickled out the door.

Carmella told our class early on, "Change your energy. Only then will you magnetize what you need into your life." Now I believed her.

Chapter 24

MONSIGNOR

I'd progressed from mocking up a gleaming penny to a serene HOA meeting. Now *that* was progress. Capitalizing on my new magic, I set my sights a little higher: mock up a man, both spiritual and interested in romantic love. I'd grown tired of trying to bond with the likes of an electrical engineer, a real estate agent, and a massage therapist, from whom one or both of those elements were sorely missing.

Once again, I attracted what I sought, but in the oddest form.

The headline on his dating profile stopped me cold: *51-Year-Old Santa Monica Priest Seeks Teacher.* Curious, I shot him a note:

FROM: "perfectstranger"
TO: "monsignorbidwell"
DATE: 5/17/95 10:22AM
SUBJECT: Seeking Teacher

Dear Monsignor:

When I was looking for a good church in Santa Monica, I hadn't considered a good priest. But the older I get, the more open-minded I become.

Laurie

For six days I heard nothing. Then, early the following Sunday, I received this email:

FROM: "monsignorbidwell"
TO: "perfectstranger"
DATE: 5/23/95 1:54AM
SUBJECT: Seeking Teacher

Dear friend:

I'm sorry it's taken me a few days to respond to your email, but I've been out of town at a retreat.

I'm 51, 5'9", 260 lbs. with a neat, gray beard. I'm soft-spoken, have a good sense of humor and am an empathetic listener. Friends tell me that I resemble Luciano Pavarotti (although I can't come close to matching his talent!). I primarily do historical research on liturgical issues.

I've grappled with feelings of guilt since I placed the ad. Yours is the first response that seemed "normal." I would like to get to know you better if you're willing.

I must confess that I have no experience with women, so if that is an impediment I will understand. I'd like to know more about you and will answer any questions you have about me.

Bidwell

I told him that I would write when I returned from a business trip. I needed time to think. I visited the dating site like dropping into a neighborhood bar—to enjoy some conviviality and maybe meet someone of like mind. Corresponding with a lonely priest was not part of the plan. But when I flew back to town, I found myself compelled to continue our exchange. I mean, how often does one enjoy a private audience with a priest who shares about *his* life? Besides, I needed to remind myself: Bidwell was the very spiritual man that I had mocked up.

FROM: "perfectstranger"
TO: "monsignorbidwell"
DATE: 5/30/95 1:30PM
SUBJECT: Where the Antelopes Roam

Dear Bidwell:

Back from a business trip in South Dakota, where the newspaper's hay report runs longer than the movie listings, and where antelopes, not Angelenos, do play.

I suppose I should tell you a little about myself. I'm 5'8", 133 lbs., auburn hair, green eyes, very athletic—tennis, yoga, and dancing.

So, Bidwell, what are you looking for here?

Laurie

I first encountered a "man of the cloth" in 1971, during my sophomore year studying English literature at the University of London. The Lutheran Church of England faced dwindling enrollment in its seminary. To make ends meet, it rented out rooms to American students like me. I found myself living with a small cohort of black-suited men in a 150-year-old stone edifice atop Richmond Hill, west of London. As the men sank to their knees in the chapel, I shuffled down the hall in fuzzy slippers, carrying shampoo and bubble bath in a yellow bucket.

At eighteen, I was naive enough to flirt with a Ghanaian bishop studying for his doctorate in theology. His name was Daniel, pronounced *Dan-yelle*. I loved to linger on the "y." His starched, white ministerial collar pinched the shiny black skin at the nape of his neck, and he spoke with a beautiful African/British accent. In spite of his formal presence, he often covered his face and dissolved into giggles.

On Sunday afternoons, he served me scones and cheese in his small seminary apartment, while we listened to Chopin nocturnes on his portable phonograph player. Whenever it rained, I knew where to find him. He'd pull a chair to the edge of the seminary's emerald lawn overlooking the Thames and read his Bible under a giant umbrella.

When I didn't hear back from Bidwell right away, I tried to rationalize his silence. He'd sent his first email well past midnight. Perhaps he had to sneak away after hours to use the rectory computer. The coast might not always be clear.

Then, three days later, I was relieved to find a letter in my box.

FROM: "monsignorbidwell"
TO: "perfectstranger"
DATE: 6/2/95 8:37PM
SUBJECT: Re: Where the Antelopes Roam

Dear Laurie:

I must admit that I am somewhat intimidated by your physical description. Beautiful AND athletic! Unfortunately, I am neither.

Before I go too far, let me answer your last question ("what are you looking for here?") because if we are not compatible on this issue, further communication might be unwise. There is no delicate way to approach this, so I'll just come out with it.

I've been celibate for 36 years. I've never had the experience of physical intimacy with a woman. Lately, this void in my life has become too much to bear. I would like to find a friend who would be willing to introduce me to what I've missed in a non-threatening, trusting, and discreet relationship.

I've carefully (and prayerfully) thought about this for the last several years. Obviously, I could get in my car and drive a few hours to a legal brothel in Nevada if my desire was only for a quick physical tryst. What I crave, however, is intimacy. I would like to find a bright, sensitive, gentle soul with a sense of humor and a love of life who can be a friend and confidante as well as a lover.

I'm afraid I don't have any money; I can't offer an open long-term commitment; I can't even be seen in public with a lady friend. I'm not, physically, the kind of man women fantasize over. And, probably worst of all, I've never been with a woman sexually and really don't know all of the techniques a lover should know. That said, it seems unlikely I'll really find the kind of friend I seek, especially one as desirable as you (is it OK to say that?).

If you don't want to communicate further, I will understand, although I really hope you will. What I can offer are true friendship, loyalty, a good mind, a sense of humor, and a willingness to learn your needs and desires and to fulfill them as best I can.

Bidwell

Just as he yearned to taste the pleasures of the flesh, I yearned to meet a man with an interior life, a man devoted to getting closer to God. In the past, when I invited boyfriends to church, they went grudgingly or shot back, "Oh, come on, you don't actually believe in that stuff, do you?" Bidwell offered the possibility of both spiritual depth and physical intimacy. When would I get a chance like this again?

After four days of digesting his email, I composed my reply:

FROM: "perfectstranger"
TO: "monsignorbidwell"
DATE: 6/6/95 12:57PM
SUBJECT: Boundaries

Dear Bidwell:

Now it's *my* turn to pray. Passages from your letter run through my head in yoga class, on the way to the dentist, and while on hold with a client. You addressed so many delicate issues, I don't know where to begin.

Perhaps I'll start with my impressions of you. Your writing shows candor, self-awareness, a command of language, and probably most important, sweetness. And, yes, I do find Luciano Pavarotti attractive.

My second impression is that you are in a lot of pain about how to maintain your vows yet fill this void in your life. If you feel so unhappy with your commitment to the Church, perhaps you should take a leave of absence (is there such a thing?) and explore your sensuality with a number of women.

Next, I should say, intimacy can be messy and inconvenient. It can make us do things we'd never dream of doing. Do you really want that?

Laurie

I had tried to become intimate with the Ghanaian bishop. It, too, got messy. I bought tickets to teach him about American culture, to movies like *Diary of a Mad Housewife* and *Midnight Cowboy*. Watching romantic scenes captivated him, especially the way Americans kiss.

"We don't kiss in Ghana," he explained. "Could you teach me to kiss like an American?"

Why not? What the hell! I snuck him into my room on the women's-only floor of the rectory. We stretched out on my prickly straw mattress and started to kiss. But after a few minutes, I realized that getting amorous with a bishop—and married with six kids—probably wasn't a good idea. Daniel's kissing lesson came to a sudden end.

I thought about Bidwell. He had no wife and no children. Compared with Daniel, he was pretty available. There was just the matter of his vows.

Less and less time now elapsed between our emails. His next letter came within twelve hours.

FROM: "monsignorbidwell"
TO: "perfectstranger"
DATE: 6/7/95 1:01AM
SUBJECT: Medieval demands

Dear Laurie:

I thought of you when I awoke, and you remained on my mind throughout my morning activities. You can't imagine how thrilled I was when I opened my email and there was a message from you.

Your impressions of me are insightful, but I'll have to rely on you to determine my "sweetness." May I confess that my heart fluttered when I read your words: "Yes, I do find Luciano Pavarotti attractive"?

I appreciate your comforting observations on my unsettled emotional state. I am not unhappy with my vocation, but I am unhappy, and more than a little angry, at my church's unnatural insistence on forced celibacy and emotional isolation for its most faithful sons.

I am particularly angry because there is no justification in Scripture for this policy. It was an invention of the Medieval Church which no longer wanted to be responsible for the offspring of priests.

The frustration I feel is over what to do now. I can't and won't be openly confrontational with the church and cause a public scandal. This is far removed from my basic personality. And neither can I continue to suppress the desires in me that are God-given and natural. I don't want to go to the end of my life without, at least once, experiencing the physical and emotional intimacy that is so central to our humanity.

The challenge I face is finding the woman who will be my partner in this exploration. I desire a woman who is mature and discreet; who is generous of spirit and sensuous of mind; who has the desire, and the patience, to teach an "old man" the things most men learn in their youth.

You don't happen to know such a woman, do you?

Bidwell

TO: “monsignorbidwell”
FROM: “perfectstranger”
DATE: 6/8/95 10:21AM
SUBJECT: Fantasies

Dear Bidwell:

It’s fun to flirt and flatter each other, but, of course, the truth is we are strangers. And we have to come to grips with that fact. Can we meet?

Laurie

He replied the same day.

TO: “perfectstranger”
FROM: “monsignorbidwell”
DATE: 6/8/95 3:10PM
SUBJECT: Perfect Strangers Make Exciting Lovers

Dear Laurie:

Do you know that feeling when you’ve made the mental decision to do something “naughty” and you experience the exhilarating tingle of excitement mingled with guilt? That is the feeling I got as I read your email to me.

I am excited by the thought that you would agree to meet me.

If we met outside my parish, it would be reasonably safe to meet in public. Even in the unlikely event that we ran into one of my parishioners, I could introduce you as “my cousin.” The danger would be in being seen regularly, as if we were dating. I assume that if you and I agreed on a sexual liaison that you have a private place we could go, making frequent public meetings unnecessary.

I would love to talk on the phone first, but it would be unwise and awkward for us to talk on the rectory phone. I want to get to know you better, Laurie. You have brought a sexual electricity to my life that I didn't think possible. I fantasize about being with you.

Bidwell

Now what? I decided to walk to the beach to collect my thoughts. Thankfully, the incessant sunshine was beginning to fade. Brought up under the grayer horizons of Ohio, I strained for the shadows, always hiding from the persistent blue skies and glare of Southern California. I yearned for the obscure and silent, while those around me thrived on sunshine and din.

The twilight and ocean lapping at my toes helped me to address my most pressing question: What the heck was I doing with Monsignor Bidwell? His willingness to risk his calling felt fresh and alluring. I had the feeling I could fall in love with him. And that was something I rarely, if ever, felt. But how could I pry a priest from his commitment? And what if I did? His sacrifice would forever haunt our union. Flirting with a priest had been a huge mistake. I vowed to end our correspondence when I got home.

But when I opened my email account to write the "Dear John" letter, I found a note waiting for me.

TO: "perfectstranger"
FROM: "monsignorbidwell"
DATE: 6/9/95 1:47PM
SUBJECT: Meeting

Dear Laurie:

I've been struggling to figure out how we might meet. What do you think about breakfast at Coffee Fix? It has a small private back patio. It's at 1023B Montana Avenue in Santa Monica, if you want to check it out.

Bidwell

Part of me was pleased that he had taken the initiative. But another part felt nothing good could come of this meeting. I had no interest in becoming a sex worker who provides "the girlfriend experience," a service for which call girls charge extra. I decided to pray.

I knelt at my altar, my grandmother's hope chest. I lit a candle and an incense stick. In my daily prayers and meditation, I could love God and feel His love with a ferocity that I rarely experienced with paramours. And I could often glean answers that I found nowhere else.

Here I am, God, caught yet again in this muddy vortex of sex, romance, and the divine. Dr. Deva wanted sex without love. Francisco offered his clients a happy ending but chose divine *over human love. Now Bidwell wants love and sex, but only on the down low, not as part of a relationship with a future. What should I do? Why do I find sex, love, spirituality, and commitment so disconnected? Don't they all fit together?*

God replied, *The monsignor has found divine communion. This might be your most profound commonality, one that you've found so lacking in past boyfriends. Experienced in loving the divine, you two are well prepared to love each other. A one-hour coffee couldn't hurt to see if this is possible.*

I got up off my knees and walked to my computer.

TO: "monsignorbidwell"
FROM: "perfectstranger"
DATE: 6/9/95 8:30PM
SUBJECT: Re: Meeting

Dear Bidwell:

The place you suggested sounds perfect. How about the morning of Friday, June 20th?

Laurie

He responded later that evening.

TO: "perfectstranger
FROM: "monsignorbidwell"
DATE: 6/9/95 10:15PM
SUBJECT: Counting the Days
Dear Laurie:

Let's plan to meet at 10 a.m. on the 20th. I'll get there a few minutes early and secure a table. I assume I'll be the only middle-aged Pavarotti look-alike in the place, so spotting me won't be hard. I have it in my appointment book and will literally be counting the hours. I don't know how I'm going to keep my mind off thoughts of you for the next 11 days!

Bidwell

Several days before our date, he wrote one last email:

TO: "perfectstranger"
FROM: "monsignorbidwell"
DATE: 6/17/95 9:54PM
SUBJECT: Mysteries

Dear Laurie:

I just want to let you know, Laurie, that my sexual desires are so strong, and my need to experience sex is so intense, that I do fantasize about you in a sexual way. I'm sure that will only increase when I actually get to see you and hear your voice and see your smile and look into your eyes.

I secretly hope that I could, perhaps, learn the mysteries of physical intimacy with you, but I come to our meeting with no expectations. So as not to offend you, I will leave the initiation of such matters to you. Be assured, Laurie, that I would willingly and eagerly accept if you offer, but I will not broach the subject.

Bidwell

Talk about pressure! No expectations, really? I could barely sleep the night before our meeting. When I got up, bleary-eyed, I pondered my wardrobe. What do you wear on a first date with a priest? I settled on a chenille sweater in ecclesiastical red—body-skimming to highlight my breasts, but not call-girl tight. I regretted that I hadn't taken the time to get my nails done. Bidwell hadn't gone on a date in thirty-six years, and I couldn't show up with a manicure?

Since Coffee Fix was just six blocks away, I decided to walk. That way I could relax a bit and get in the mood. But I headed out the door with only ten minutes to spare. My leisurely stroll quickly turned into a power walk and then a trot. As I waited for the light to turn green at a crosswalk, I was panting and sweaty.

I stood outside the café, bent over, my hands braced against my knees, trying to catch my breath. I'd hoped to look cool and confident when I made my entrance. As I stepped into the secluded courtyard, I spotted Bidwell. He *did* look like Pavarotti, just a whole lot bigger. He sat in the corner, in tortoiseshell half-glasses, reading *The New York Times*.

Sensing someone was watching him, he lowered the paper to just below eye level, and studied me, like a spy on surveillance. "Laurie?" he mouthed.

I didn't want my face to reveal anything but pleasure at seeing him. To hide my disappointment at his size, I went into coquette mode. I walked over, leaned in, and in my most sultry voice whispered, "Hello, Cousin Bidwell."

He smiled and pulled out the chair next to him without getting up. As I sat down, I noticed that he wore black slacks and a black V-neck sweater over a laurel green polo shirt. He had a thick head of curly salt-and-pepper hair and a closely trimmed beard. Even though he'd carefully shaved from the bottom edge of his beard to below his shirt line, a few black chest hairs poked through the button holes of his shirt.

He turned toward me in his seat, tilted his head to the side and intertwined his thick fingers.

"Are you going to take my confession?" I asked him with a smile.

He hesitated. "No, but you've taken mine."

"Have I?"

"Well, I've confessed more to you than to any of my fellow priests, friends, and family members over the past decade."

His eyes, for a moment, slid down to take in my breasts. For a man who claimed inexperience with women, he was doing a pretty good job of flirting.

The waitress arrived. He ordered black coffee, and I, eggs and hash browns.

I looked around the courtyard. "This café is a find. So quiet and secluded."

"Yes, it reminds me of Rome. I have an apartment at the Vatican."

I raised my eyebrows.

He nodded, pleased that he'd impressed me. "I consider Rome my home base."

Stunned, I realized that I'd underestimated him. A priest who lives part-time at the Vatican must have risen high up in the church.

"Do you get to wear anything you want on your day off?" I asked cheerily, trying to steer the conversation to less weighty topics.

"There's no dress code," he said. "Some of the priests look like they're headed for the golf course. And some are. But I like to dress conservatively."

"All black?"

"Well, I can wear any color except red. Like I couldn't wear the color you're wearing." He eyed my breasts again. "Only cardinals can wear red. But truth be told, there are some mornings I look at myself in the mirror and think, 'Hmmm, I'd look good in scarlet!'"

"Do you want to be a cardinal?" I asked, trying to gauge his ambition. A cardinal-in-waiting would never stray too far from the fold. I didn't want to relive *The Thorn Birds*.

"As a liturgical historian, I'm too much of a specialist. I think the Church is looking for generalists to become cardinals—someone with more pastoral and financial management experience."

As he talked, he smiled at regular intervals, regardless of where he was in the conversation.

"Stop me if I'm boring you," he said. "That's the trouble with being a priest all your life, you're used to preaching at people. You don't necessarily develop good reciprocal social skills."

"Our conversation flows just as easily as our emails," I assured him. But what I wanted to say was, *Hey buddy, you haven't asked me a single question. What's up with that?* Like many men I met, Bidwell was eager to access my body. But to actually learn about me? Not so much. *Forget about moves in the bedroom,* I wanted to tell him. *Your first lesson should be in the art of reciprocal conversation.* Who wants to bed a man who displays absolutely no curiosity about his partner?

I stuck my fork in my hash browns and took a bite, giving him a chance to initiate the next train of thought. By the time I finished chewing, he hadn't said anything. I continued with my line of questioning, my default setting as a journalist. "You said my response to your initial email was the only 'normal' one. Why was that?"

"Some of the responses were just plain kinky. About a dozen of the respondents were homosexual. Others were vulnerable women who had been hurt and looked to me as someone safe to be with, someone who would be there for them in a way that others had not."

Maybe I'm one of the vulnerable women, too, I thought. *I just hide it better.*

"I was discouraged . . . until I met you," he said.

In spite of my concern about his conversational deficiencies, I felt giddy. He liked me! Then I felt panic. My duties as a sex teacher felt frighteningly imminent. I needed more time.

"What led you to become a priest in the first place?" For a man so hell-bent on breaking into the carnal world, I wondered about his initial impetus to lead a life of celibacy.

"I grew up in a big Catholic family in New York City, one of eight children. It wasn't unusual for the best and the brightest sons to choose the priesthood, as I did at fifteen."

"Just like that?"

"Our family lived in a small house. There wasn't much privacy. In the seminary I had my own room. So that was one big advantage of the priesthood. Plus, the Church sent me to Georgetown to earn a master's degree in ancient history and to the Vatican for postgraduate studies."

To me, the benefits of the priesthood sounded like the GI Bill. "So why now? Why choose now for a liaison? There must have been plenty of opportunities, at Georgetown and in Rome."

"At thirty-one, I could barely contain my passions. The same was true at forty-one. I was afraid if I tried to develop a relationship with a woman, the lure would be too great, that I would leave the Church, which meant so much to me."

"And now?"

"At fifty-one, with a more tempered libido, I feel I'm more in control of my passions. I believe I can keep that part of my life separate from my pastoral duties."

He studied my face, which gave away nothing. I'd learned the impassive expression of a journalist, just as he had the opacity of a priest.

Inside, though, my anger was mounting. Bidwell was saying he could keep me in a sealed box, never to spill over into his other, more important life. He reminded me of Dr. Deva, who had also put sex in a box, treating it like an inebriant, divested from love and a long-term relationship.

Once again, I steered our exchange to smoother waters. "How has your summer been?" I asked.

"June has always been my toughest month," he said. "That's when my parishioners send me postcards. They're building sandcastles with their kids. Bicycling with their wife through Ireland. Snorkeling in the Red Sea with their lover. All of a sudden, the rectory library gets very dark. Something about the angle of the sun this time of year. I reposition my chair throughout the day to follow that one splash of light on my page." He looked off into the distance.

I then felt sorry for Bidwell. He'd chosen a life of supreme contemplation . . . and captivity. "What do you research in the library?"

"Right now, I'm researching the role of the Catholic Church in the Holocaust. The cardinals want to know the real story even if they have no intention of ever making it public. I've spent the past ten years off and on researching at the Vatican Library."

Turned out Bidwell was a lot like me in that we both liked to ferret out and decode secrets. But our one-sided conversation was pissing me off. I found him fascinating; I wanted him to find me fascinating, too.

He looked at me, and I thought he was going to ask me a question. When he didn't, I asked, as calmly as I could, "What's the Vatican Library like?"

"Two rooms are devoted to nothing but the Inquisition. Another to the execution of Joan of Arc. I'd do anything to look inside those rooms. But the doors have these one-foot-square wax seals that only a cardinal can break."

The Catholic Church harbored more secrets than any lover I'd ever had.

Bidwell continued. "There are these leather-bound notebooks of original research performed by the Jesuit brothers before me. It's great material, representing a lifetime of work, but they have never been read—except maybe by a couple of cardinals."

We fell silent; then he asked, "So what are you looking for, Laurie?" It was the first question he'd asked about me. Our thirty minutes of conversation, or rather our Q&A, had been nothing but polite small talk, a prelude to this primary query: Was I willing to fill that empty compartment in his life?

When I didn't answer, he gently asked, "Do you want to get married?"

"Yes," I said slowly, afraid that my answer might be the deal-breaker. I realized it was now or never to rework his proposition into a more palatable one for me. "You know, what you want doesn't exist—a call girl and a genuine girlfriend simultaneously."

"Am I on a fool's quest?"

"Bidwell," I said quietly, "we're cut from the same cloth. I think we could get involved. But I worry that you wouldn't be open to wherever that might lead."

He was silent for a long time. "You know, you might be right, but . . ."

"But what?"

"The church has been my whole life. It's all I've known."

"I understand. It's impossible to walk away from that." I hoped he'd contradict me.

"You know what I think, Laurie? You're so charming and pretty, you'll fall madly in love with a man who isn't encumbered, who wants to be with you all the time."

I didn't bother to point out that I'd been waiting a long time for such a thing to happen. "And you?"

"I'll put aside my sensual and sexual needs and realize what I have with the Church."

I suspected he was just expressing polite words after a deal gone bad. He'd laid out his proposition. I hadn't gone for it. End of story. I felt piercingly disappointed.

The waitress cleared our plates. Bidwell turned down her offer of more coffee and opened his wallet to pay the check. Looking back at me, he asked, "Have I satisfied your curiosity, Laurie?"

I winced. Maybe that's what I'd been all along—a curiosity seeker. I'd had to deceive Bidwell *and* myself to satisfy my inquisitiveness. Deep down, I knew there was no hope of luring a priest from his thirty-six-year commitment to the Catholic Church.

Out on the sidewalk, the street brightly lit and bustling with shoppers, Bidwell held out his hand, large and warm and soft. It was the first time we'd touched each other.

"So long, Laurie."

Our breakfast had been a take-it-or-leave-it proposition. In all likelihood, I would never see him again.

He unlocked his white subcompact. The car rocked with his weight as he hoisted himself into the driver's seat. I thought of his years of sublimated appetites and my years of yearning for someone just like him. We waved to each other as I crossed the street.

Back in my home office, I could feel the tension of our six-week correspondence slowly lift. We were no longer a figment of each other's imagination. I didn't have to worry about our impending meeting; it had already transpired.

Still, I was too riled up to start working. I donned sneakers and headed out for a walk. What the heck had just happened? Why did I have a sense of déjà vu?

The Ghanaian bishop had wanted kissing lessons. The Indian guru had wanted a twelve-hour Tantric sex session. The yoga teacher had wanted a free place to crash. A Catholic priest, a liturgical historian no less, now wanted me to teach an old dog new tricks.

I focused on the happy lessons I'd learned, albeit with caveats. I liked that I attracted spiritual men, even if most of the time I appealed to just their carnal side. I liked my sense of adventure, even though some might call it foolhardiness. I liked my open-mindedness, even though one friend observed, "That can mean empty-headedness." And I liked my capacity to say no to situations that proved unwise, even if it *did* take me six months to say no to the yogi sleeping on my foldout couch. I wasn't a pushover, at least not over the long haul.

Even though none of these associations had translated to a long-term union or even a friendship, maybe I could change that pattern. Maybe I could stay in touch with Bidwell, even if it meant just an occasional dispatch from the Vatican.

That night, after finishing my client work, I gingerly went online to see if he'd sent an email. Relieved, I saw that he had.

TO: "perfectstranger"
FROM: "monsignorbidwell"
DATE: 6/19/95 11:47PM
SUBJECT: My last kiss

Dear Laurie:

You should know that my only sexual experience occurred when I was 15, in the summer before I left home for the seminary. I was at a dance and spent the evening with a girl my age, whom I had admired throughout the summer. We danced together most of the evening. I can still smell her perfume and feel the way she felt in my arms! Toward the end of the evening, we took a walk outside the school gym where the dance was held. We sat on a bench by the school track. We talked and held hands. I leaned toward her, and we kissed. My God, it was thirty-six years ago, and I still get a thrill at the memory! We kissed for a while, and it became quite passionate. I touched her breast and felt her nipple harden through the thin material of her summer dress.

About that point, her father, who was chaperoning the dance, came out of the gym looking for us. At the end of the evening, she kissed me on the cheek. The next morning, I left for the seminary and celibacy.

It was a beautiful experience, and the memory has lasted a lifetime.

Bidwell

I was pleased that he still wanted to talk to me, and so intimately . . . especially since his goodbye seemed so final. I dashed off a reply.

TO: “monsignorbidwell”
FROM: “perfectstranger”
DATE: 6/20/95 6:30PM
SUBJECT: About our meeting

Dear Bidwell:

Your story is so haunting. Thank you for your willingness to share it with me. I enjoyed our breakfast. I felt our rapport was just as good in person as online.

What are your thoughts?

Laurie

When I hit “Send,” a message came on the screen: “Inactive email address.” *There must be some mistake,* I thought. I tried again. And again. I looked at the time stamp on his last email. He had sent it the night *before* our breakfast, not afterward. In my rush to get ready in the morning, I’d neglected to read his letter.

I searched for his account on the dating site. His profile had vanished. I realized I didn’t know his real name, his phone number, and now, not even his email address. Monsignor Bidwell had evaporated as quickly as he’d appeared six weeks earlier.

I was so saddened by his disappearance, I suffered a flu-like malaise for a month. And for years, Monsignor Bidwell hung in my memory, just as that girl at the dance lingered in his.

Chapter 25

GET THEE TO A CONVENT

If I couldn't lure Bidwell away from the priesthood, maybe I should join him . . . that is, in the female version, a nunnery.

During his sermon at church on Sunday, a monk mentioned a job opening. I grabbed a collection envelope in the pew to jot down the phone number of the hiring manager. The job was writing for the public affairs department of the organization's convent. Twenty miles northeast of downtown Los Angeles, the convent stood atop a mountain overlooking Altadena.

I'd quit my job at the downtown nonprofit and now worked as a freelance writer out of my bedroom above a well-tended garden. Even though I enjoyed lots of freedom and peace, I'd grown sick of the isolation . . . literally. I suffered one cold or flu after another.

And maybe I belonged in a convent. One day my mother had casually mentioned, "You know, your great-aunt served as the Mother Superior of a convent in Austria." Perhaps my aunt's blood coursed through my veins.

The public affairs director gave me a writing test: a five-hundred-word press release on a book written by the organization's leader. I procrastinated, worried that my words could never achieve the standards of a world-renowned religious organization. Eventually, I emailed my final draft and crossed my fingers. I got the job.

"You're gonna write for God!" my friends marveled. "You'll never find a better gig."

What mattered, though, was a chance to enter a convent. I yearned to rub elbows with like-minded souls on a daily basis, not just one hour a week at a Sunday morning service. Other cultures integrated religion into the warp and woof of life. Mexican families honored their ancestors at altars placed prominently in their homes. Muslims prayed five times a day, no matter where they were. Their worship contrasted markedly with the WASP Episcopal tradition I was born into: Once a week, a cerebral sermon, a few hymns sung off-key, and a struggle to make conversation with a gaggle of couples over bad coffee. I had improved my experience of organized religion in my thirties. At Sunday service, I relished meditating with my fellow parishioners, but the communality lasted only one hour a week.

On my first day of work at the convent, I navigated hairpin turns on the climb up the mountain. Drought had browned the hillsides and canyons, but when I glided through the convent's wrought iron gates and down a long drive lined with palms, the lawn glowed, each blade of grass an even shade of green.

Nuns—in pale yellow, navy, and ocher saris—smiled as I passed. I waved, pleased at their friendliness. How I longed to hear their stories. What had led them to leave family and friends, jobs and pastimes, perhaps lovers and spouses, to live in a nunnery? But my new boss warned, "Don't mingle with the monastics. You're lay staff."

Still, I caught glimpses of the renunciants. Walking to my car one evening, I came upon a nun watering giant sunflowers. "The day after I planted these seeds, my brother, in perfect health, died of a heart attack," she told me. "These sunflowers are my memorial to him. He was 6'2". So are they."

A similar magical thread wound through the monastics' emails. One read, "LOST ITEM. Importance: HIGH. I dropped a small white envelope that contained four pebbles. It is very important that I find this envelope and the stones. Thank you very much, Brahmacharini Crystal." (Before they achieved "Sister" status, all nuns were referred to as "Brahmacharini," the Sanskrit term for a devoted female student.) I so wanted to write back, "Please tell me about the pebbles." But it was obviously a private matter.

When one coworker fell ill and resigned, nuns lined up to hug her goodbye. One remarked that we could all use some "Vitamin H," her term for a hug, as she wrapped her arms around my colleague.

But mainly I hung out with the four women who worked with me in public affairs. Over vegetarian tacos in Sierra Madre and Indian fare in Pasadena, we shared our lives. When Bettina climbed into bed at night, she slipped an amber stone on her wedding ring finger. The single mother of three wanted to manifest her third husband. A few months later, during a press junket, the presiding monk, spotting Bettina, exclaimed, "So, who do we have here?" The ring had worked. He left a monastic life spanning three decades to marry her and wore the amber ring on his pinkie finger.

When Selma's watch broke, she simply taped a small paper circle over the face with "NOW" printed on it in thick black letters. "I need to remember to stay in the present moment," she explained. "That's far more important than knowing what time it is."

As the five of us worked together in tight quarters and meditated at noon in the convent chapel, an intuitive stream began to run beneath us. The advice each gave me was so spot-on, it sounded like that of a $350-an-hour therapist. "As you meditate more," Bettina pointed out, "you will feel less alienated, more assured of your place in God's creation." And she was right. Meditation made me feel less needy, less filled with yearning.

Miriam advised, "We have all these plans for what we think should happen to make us happy. But the spiritual realm often overrides our plans. It arranges circumstances in such a way that we learn the lessons we need to learn."

Certainly, the well-appointed homes I'd created in my twenties and thirties had not manifested the family I'd hoped for. Maybe it was because the universe had other plans for me, lessons of a different sort.

Midafternoon, my coworkers and I laced on tennis shoes for a walk, sometimes together, but often apart. Unlike previous employers, the convent practically mandated staff take a long break at least once a day.

I'd head out to the convent gardens, starting at the pond outside the door of the administration building. Half-open pink lotus blossoms, the Hindu symbol of the awakening soul, floated on the black surface. A large gold koi glided toward me, hoping for a treat. A nun in a pale yellow sari drifted by a private walkway. To my surprise, she waved and called out "hello" in what sounded like a foreign accent. The monastic community attracted novitiates and employees from all over the world. She flashed a glorious smile and then disappeared.

From the pond, I strolled into the gardens, dotted with streams and birdbaths. A hummingbird drank from a blossom tumbling from an arbor. A man meditated on a bench in a courtyard, as a large calico cat peered out from his canvas satchel.

The gardens opened to an unlikely sight: a tennis court. I wondered if the monks and nuns played a vigorous round of doubles when the grounds closed to the public.

Beyond the courts, a vast expanse of lawn stretched out to the convent gates. Nuns walked their dogs—golden retrievers, dachshunds, German shepherds—pulling every which way on their leashes. I giggled at the sight. These women lived a highly disciplined life of daily meditation, prayer, and spiritual study, yet they apparently had little control over their hounds. Sometimes one broke loose, raced through the public affairs office, and rifled through my wastebasket, searching for a sandwich wrapper. I'd page the owner: "Brahmacharini Helen, I've got Charlie."

Once a colleague arranged a private tour for me of the former quarters of the founding guru. The small bedroom and sitting room on the third floor of the convent's administration building were filled with hand-carved cabinets, jade figurines, and a collection of large, uncut stones—amethysts, tourmalines, and amber—gifts from visiting dignitaries. The windows captured the late afternoon sun and misty views of hills. I knelt at the guru's bedside to pray, hoping to buy myself a little more time, as my escort lingered in the dark hall. The bedspread was a glittery gold lamé. I suspected it had been a postmortem add-on, not the founder's choice of decoration. Kneeling there at his single bed, I felt this centeredness, depth and a strange mix of ecstasy and calm. His spirit had been so strong, it lingered decades after his death in 1937.

That feeling persisted, not just for a few minutes, but for days. I loved it so much I wanted to return. But my private tour had been rare, monastics told me, not to be repeated, at least not anytime soon.

I felt as though I'd fallen into this secret, privileged club—what I imagined a good marriage must be like. In fact, many of the nuns wore wedding rings to signify their marriage to God. The nuns spent a considerable time "on the other side," experiencing the love of God. As a result, their company felt like a contact high. I could breathe in their divine communion. By contrast, the carnal world felt jarring; I often had to protect myself from others' negative energy fields. For the first time in my life, I felt in sync with my surroundings. Others' essences fed me, rather than depleting me.

Chapter 26

COME CLOSER

I began to explore how I might take my vows. To understand the hierarchy, I asked coworkers why the nuns wore different colors. "Navy is for the novitiates," Bettina explained. "Pale yellow is for the next level of Brahmacharini. Ocher is for when you take your final vows and become a Sister."

"But what about white?" A smattering of nuns wore bright white saris.

"Those are for the women who enter the convent at thirty-five or older," she said. "They are viewed as so embedded in the carnal world—you know, getting married, having children, assuming mortgages—that they can never achieve true renunciation and the transcendence that promises."

"They never progress to yellow and ocher?"

"No, they're always in white."

"So permanently second-string?"

"I never thought of it like that, but yes, they're never completely accepted in the fold."

At forty-four, I could join the second-string white order. But could I hack the renunciation of worldly possessions, family, and friends? I imagined reading bootlegged *New Yorkers* under the covers and hiding the latest draft of a short story in my underpants drawer. Maybe the order was right. Like a tree irrevocably trained by the carnal world, I couldn't bend to the demands of a nunnery.

Besides, there were troubling signs. At one of our weekly lunches, coworkers whispered that some monastics had been requesting psychological counseling, a brave request considering that the teachings mandated that all problems be addressed through prayer and meditation.

Then there was my boss. As I got to know Daphne, her true character unfolded. One day, I ducked my head in her office to ask a quick question. She sat behind a giant mahogany desk, red-faced, wild-eyed, engulfed in tall piles of files. Clearly, she was immersed in her drug of choice: frantic busyness to keep her pumped with adrenaline and shore up her fragile ego: *Look at how productive I am!*

"Yes?" Daphne asked breathlessly. I felt embarrassed, like I'd walked in on her shooting heroin.

"I can see you're busy." I beat a quick retreat.

Even though public affairs, by definition, is about communication, Boss Lady seemed incapable of this essential element of the profession. At weekly meetings, she spoke nonstop. Neither I nor any colleague could get a word in edgewise. To make matters worse, she was more apt to criticize than to praise our performance.

"Daphne doesn't converse," Selma explained; "she dominates." Bettina said bluntly, "The atmosphere, when Daphne's here, is filled with suspicion, caution, coldness, and meanness. That's unhealthy for all of us to be around."

Daphne's behavior contrasted sharply with the convent's loving, bucolic ambience. That conflict left me forever jockeying between two very different settings: on the one hand, as porous as possible, to absorb the divine bliss of the convent, and on the other hand, girding myself against Daphne's toxicity.

"A convent is a home for troubled souls," Neville pointed out one night. "Your boss is troubled. So are you, just in a different way."

Neville was right. My boss yearned to shore up her fragile ego. I yearned, too, but for something else. Like Francisco, I wanted to give and receive love. And, like Francisco, I was slowly discovering the divine realm provided a better venue to do that, far more than romance ever had.

The convent had housed soldiers convalescing during World War I. Perhaps the convent had remained a sanitarium; only now, as Neville observed, it served as a hospital for sick souls.

I avoided Daphne as best I could. My desk was not within earshot or eyeshot of hers. Thank God. Then one day, she ordered that I move my desk outside her door.

"Daphne doesn't get you," my colleagues explained. "You're a wild card. Moving you close by is her way of dominating someone she hasn't been able to understand and control."

I whispered to Bettina as I lugged my computer to the new cubicle, "'Come closer,' said the spider to the fly."

To help dissipate Daphne's vortex of negativity, I bought elegant desk accessories: an architect-designed lime-green tape dispenser from Museum of Modern Art, a see-through turquoise stapler, and an orange-and-yellow plexiglass business card holder. But even these artful accoutrements didn't work. One by one, my coworkers resigned and, as I neared my three-year anniversary, so did I.

Bettina was sanguine about the disbandment of our tight-knit group. "We came together for a time because we had something to teach each other. Now we've used up that learning experience, so it's time to say goodbye."

After the office emptied at 5 p.m., I ventured into parts of the convent that were off-limits to lay staff, where only the monastics were allowed. I stole through the halls. In certain pockets, I felt lightheaded, elated, almost drugged, similar to my experience visiting the guru's tiny third-floor bedroom. Even in the monastics' absence, I could breathe in their divine union. The vibe contrasted with what I experienced in the real world. How could I rejoin that world, knowing the vast difference?

I filled my backpack with my cherished desk accessories, swung the bag over my shoulder and headed out the convent door for the last time. A few lights dotted the top floor of the building. They would soon grow dark. The nuns went to bed after an early dinner.

I passed through the wrought iron gates. The cool breeze stilled, and the air grew hotter. I inched down the one hundred steps to the parking lot.

It was hard to believe I would never again see that particular stretch of the hillside—bathed in the pink light of morning or the long golden rays of evening. I gazed at the image to sear it in my mind. As I did, I saw something I'd never noticed before. One small square of the hillside, one person's lawn, popped; it was a brighter green than the rest. Perhaps that neighbor watered, fertilized, and reseeded their grass more. I wound down the mountain road to the freeway. At a stop sign, I gazed out at the city lights, sparkling in the distance. At that moment, I vowed to be that square of bright green in the world.

Chapter 27

MATERIAL WORLD

Despite my misgivings, I hopped back into the material world with both feet, trading the convent for a business magazine in a sunbaked office park. My office no longer overlooked a fountain edged with flowers. Instead, I typed away in a windowless, cinder block bunker about the size of a prison cell.

The CEO, whom we all called Geoff, had made millions as a business consultant. The magazine was simply his vanity project, a way to promote himself as a small-business guru. The only problem was, he had no idea how to run a small business, least of all his own.

His ineptitude, my office mate John explained, may have had something to do with his drug habit. "He's constantly sniffing, girl."

"Yeah, and those fits he flies into . . ."

"Uh huh, it's the coke."

Geoff, in a high state of animation, led motivational meetings, tossing rolls of $20 bills to rows of employees like dog treats. One day, when John happened to catch the prize, he pretended it was a hot potato and tossed it to me.

"John, there's $240 here!" I said, unrolling the bills on his desk. "They're yours. You caught them first."

He laughed. "You take 'em. You deserve it."

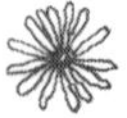

As Geoff's addiction accelerated, so did his harebrained ideas. Rather than host the company picnic at one of the many parks in the San Fernando Valley, he ordered an eighteen-wheeler to deliver a ton of sand to the staff cafeteria. We donned bathing suits and picnicked on the makeshift beach, while a cassette of ocean wave sounds played on a boom box.

Dust from the sand hung in the air for weeks. My colleagues and I laughed as we passed in the hall, wildly waving our hands to clear a path through the cloud.

Eventually, subscribers to the magazine caught on that Geoff was not the small-business guru he claimed to be. Many canceled their subscriptions. One even included a dildo with his cancellation card to illustrate the depth of his pique. Not long after, Geoff began to issue pink slips to one employee after another.

I dimmed the overhead lights and cranked up my positive ion machine, which now did double duty. It reduced the increasing toxicity of the environment, and it drowned out phone calls I started to place to prospective employers. If Geoff happened to wander in, he wouldn't overhear my quest for another job.

To make matters worse, I was turning forty-five in two months. I felt like a prison door was about to clang shut behind me. In my mind, this birthday spelled the end of my dream of getting married.

I decided a vacation might do me good, give me some much-needed perspective. I booked a ten-day jaunt to Patzcuaro, Mexico, known for its celebration of Day of the Dead on November 1 and 2.

"I need to get away," I told John. "Maybe just as important, I need to prove to myself that I can travel solo."

"Why's that?"

"I've missed way too many vacations waiting to share them with the right sweetheart," I explained. "I'm done waiting."

My first morning in Patzcuaro, I took a taxi into town, past white-washed adobe houses, a tangle of bright purple bougainvillea spilling over courtyard walls. At the town plaza, I immediately felt drawn to the cathedral.

Inside, I took a seat in the front pew. Rose petals dotted the aisle, perhaps from a wedding the night before. Squat women left their groceries at the door, knelt at the altar, then, collecting their bags, continued with their daily routine. Through the windows, I could see people sweeping gravestones in the cemetery in preparation for the evening Day of the Dead party. Just as going to church was woven into their daily errands, so, it appeared, the dead were included in life.

At 8 p.m. on Day of the Dead, I took a bus to Janitzio, an island in the middle of a lake, famous for its cemetery. At midnight, the graveyard was almost as bright as day, lit with thousands of votive candles. Families shared picnics on beach blankets spread across tiny grave plots or monstrous mausoleums. Vendors sold *pan de muerte*, an egg bread in the shape of a skeleton, decorated with white frosting to look like twisted bones. Pillows had been propped against tombstones so the deceased could rest after their long journey from the Great Beyond. It was one big party. I bathed in the orange light and the warmth of community.

Back in my hotel room, I couldn't sleep. Perhaps some spirits had followed me to deliver the lessons of the night. I grabbed my diary and tried to make sense of my jangled thoughts.

> *Obviously, I was born in the wrong culture, the wrong country. I yearn for the far more immersive experience that religion provides to Patzcuarans. In the absence of that community, I will have to marshal spiritual momentum on my own. Yeah, it would be nice to have a husband and home filled with family. But, in the absence of that, I will need to forge a different kind of cohesion, a different kind of support system.*

I shut my diary. The getaway had given me the perspective, albeit harsh, that I needed.

Two days later, I returned to my dark cinder block office. I reached down below my desk to turn on my computer. But I couldn't find the tower.

"Switch on the overheads," I ordered John.

He quickly snapped on the lights as if prepared for my request.

I knelt under my desk. My hard drive was gone.

"Human Resources said to see them when you came in," he said sheepishly.

"I'm next, aren't I?"

He nodded. "I'm so sorry."

A security guard stood watch while I packed my belongings. It felt surreal to morph from trusted employee to criminal suspect. I boxed up everything I had collected over the years but left the positive ion machine for John.

"Thanks, I'll need it," he said.

"I'm going to miss you," I told him.

"Me, too. But I won't be far behind you. I bet I'm next on the chopping block."

"Can I at least say goodbye to my other colleagues?" I asked the security guard.

"No, you must go now."

I slowly made my way down the hall. The guard trailed behind, carrying my posters and the large cardboard box of my belongings. With a loud clang, he dropped the box in the trunk of my car.

As I drove away, I felt banished, like I'd been ushered onto a slab of ice to drift out to sea.

Back home, I recalled Oleg, the Russian defector I'd befriended when I first moved to LA. I felt his dislocation. Suddenly separated from my employer and friends, I could empathize with Oleg's crossing the Yugoslavian border, leaving behind his girlfriend, widowed mother, and country forever.

A few years after Oleg and I parted ways in 1985, something happened that neither of us—nor most global citizens—could have predicted. In November 1989, the Berlin Wall fell. Oleg could return to his homeland, enjoy its new unfettered capitalism, and, who knows, reunite with his beautiful Slavic girlfriend.

On a whim, in late 1989, I stopped by Oleg's apartment building and scanned the resident directory in the lobby. When I couldn't find his name, I pushed all the buttons at once. Only one neighbor answered on the building's intercom.

Oleg had moved to Las Vegas, the man explained. "He's making a killing at the craps table, I've heard. Something about dice control. Changes your odds, I guess."

As I drove home that evening, I punched my fist in the air. Oleg had rallied. He had bucked one almost impenetrable system—defecting from communist Russia—and now he was bucking another: the law of probability. He was thriving within his own rarefied fiefdom.

What a role model. That's exactly what I needed to do now: carve out a new fiefdom tailored just for me. Suddenly I remembered that bright green lawn on the hillside by the convent—the one that stood out from the rest.

Chapter 28

DEAR PRINCESS

Fortunately, my secret networking had paid off. After the Christmas holidays, I started a new job at the local school district as a press agent for their volunteer program. I liked writing profiles to recruit more volunteers for the cash-strapped district. The job combined my writing skills with my need to serve the most vulnerable. That felt like an improvement in my career trajectory.

On the downside, I now worked alongside bureaucrats, not creatives like at the magazine. I no longer dwelt with my own kind, my own tribe.

I decided yet again I needed the perspective that Patzcuaro had delivered. So, for spring break in 1997, I booked a flight halfway around the world. I hoped Thailand would deliver similar fresh insight.

✻

After one week of bicycling through the Golden Triangle, I stopped in Bangkok to recuperate and tour the city. My first morning, I hailed a cab to the attraction I didn't want to miss—Temple of the

Reclining Buddha, the gold, 150-foot-long statue that represented Buddha's entry into nirvana and the end of all reincarnation. If that vision wasn't mind-blowing enough, the four chapels in the compound featured almost four hundred additional Buddhas. I bought little pieces of gold leaf that I stuck to the statue. In the early morning light, they shimmered as they waved back and forth in the sun.

When I spotted an astrologer selling readings, I jumped at the chance. If any place emanated divine wisdom, this one did. So what if he smoked a hand-rolled cigarette throughout the reading. He told me that I would marry soon—perhaps the stock prediction he delivered to every woman traveling alone in Bangkok.

No matter. When I got home, I signed up for the dating service Match.com to take advantage of my perfect planetary alignment.

I received dozens of emails but knew enough not to be flattered. Such attention was given to all newcomers. I dismissed most of the correspondents as incompatible, until I heard from a San Diegan named CelebratesSpirit, a forty-eight-year-old also from the Cleveland area. Jonathan hailed from the "other side of the tracks," the blue-collar suburb of Berea, while I had grown up in Gates Mills, a community of sprawling estates and polo fields.

"My mother warned me about those boys from Berea," I wrote.

A software engineer, Jonathan quickly indoctrinated me into the newfangled technology of ICQ ("I seek you"), an early form of instant messaging. ICQ compensated for my shyness and capitalized on my inclination toward the written rather than the spoken word. Our online banter got me high. I began our exchange this way:

So, tell me, why's your handle CelebratesSpirit?
Seven years ago, I died in a fiery car crash.

So, am I talking to a ghost?
No, paramedics revived me.

Phew.
I had a near-death experience. The Universe gave my life back to me, but on one condition.

Which was?
That I teach people on Earth how to love. In this capacity, God assigned me the role of "Senator of the Spiritual Realm."

How's that going?

I wondered if I was talking to a nut.

It's harder than I thought.

Because?
My ten-year marriage ended and I'm dating again. What I'm finding is that so many singles aren't healthy. There's alcoholism, childhood abuse, and lots of anger.

Oh?
And men are about 100 years behind women in emotional development. So, women eventually get jaded and harder to reach.

Our subsequent texts and emails quickly grew in candor and intimacy. After one week of daily correspondence, I sent him this message:

I enjoy our communication, Jonathan, but keep in mind, we still haven't met.
What if we met in a bar and knew exactly how the other looked? Would we know each other better than with what we're doing now—learning what's inside each of us?

Since we lived 150 miles apart, we decided to meet halfway between Los Angeles and San Diego at the train station in San Juan Capistrano. Then we planned to take a short drive to the Ramakrishna Monastery. I checked the train schedule, then told him I'd be arriving on the 4:40 p.m. train, wearing my favorite garnet-red velvet scarf so he could spot me.

After a minute of jostling with the passengers pouring onto the train platform, Jonathan tapped my shoulder. I turned around and recognized his face from his Match.com profile. He had pale green eyes, a pixie smile, and a misshapen little finger, perhaps a casualty of his car crash. He seemed surprisingly boyish, especially for a twice-married father of two. And, like a young boy, tongue-tied.

After our intimate ICQ exchanges, we had advanced beyond polite pleasantries. Yet, as people meeting for the first time, a more intimate exchange seemed inappropriate.

Thank goodness we had plans to do something. It would be better than sitting opposite each other in a loud restaurant struggling to make conversation.

We drove in silence in his Toyota Camry, winding uphill to the Ramakrishna Monastery. I assured myself that we just needed time to get to know each other.

Walking through the woods outside the Hindu monastery, along a trail featuring shrines to world religions, we stopped and meditated at the Dharma Wheel of Buddhism. But I was so distracted by his presence, I couldn't focus. Jonathan seemed tightly wound, as if there was something lurking beneath the surface that could erupt at any moment. That potential both intrigued and frightened me.

We moved on, twirled the Medicine Wheel of the Native Americans, and identified the Om symbol dangling in the air as that of Hinduism. I smiled to myself at the "SILENCE, PLEASE" signs posted regularly on trees. *No problem on that score,* I thought. Although we had communicated incessantly in ICQ chats, we seemed clueless about what to say to each other in person. No matter. Even in the absence of charming banter, I felt strangely elated in his presence.

"That's what's known as chemistry," Neville informed me later. Finding chemistry was such a rare experience for me, I couldn't even identify it.

We stopped for banana bread and coffee at Starbucks shortly before I caught the train back to LA. Noticing foam on my lips as I sipped my cappuccino, Jonathan leaned over and kissed me. "Now we have matching mustaches!" he said.

We laughed. Our first kiss wasn't awkward at all. We sat sipping our coffee in silence, smiling at each other. He wasn't fidgety or distracted by other customers. He didn't check his watch. He was totally still and present with me. That was such a relief, especially considering my pet peeve: men with short attention spans.

Equally appealing, we seemed to share the same preferred speed. Like me, he pursued everything—ideas or activities—slowly and quietly. That felt completely antithetical to LA's kinetic and loud rhythm.

As I studied Jonathan, I noticed a slight hunch in his back. I drew my fingers over the curve.

"My back's held together with steel pins," he said. "You know, from the car crash."

"It makes you look like a wizened survivor," I whispered. "Maybe like the 'Senator of the Spiritual Realm.'"

He smiled. "You remembered."

"I'm so curious what you learned when you died."

"I learned that you need to plug into the divine first and foremost for your source of power, and stop plugging into things, people, and situations for your main conduit of energy."

Before I could respond, a whistle blew in the distance. It was the 9:50 p.m. train, the last one of the evening. We slid out of the booth and crossed the street to wait on the platform. As the train came to a stop, Jonathan hopped on board, climbing a few steps leading up to the car.

"Are you coming with me?"

He smiled, kissed the palm of my hand, and leapt off just as the train picked up speed.

I looked out the window as the sleeping cities slipped by. I was excited at the prospect of getting to know Jonathan, but at the same time I wondered what I was doing with the guy. I reviewed all that he had shared about himself in our week of texting. He'd been divorced twice. He'd just gotten out of a ten-year marriage. He cared for his two young sons every other weekend. And he lived 150 miles away. This relationship was probably not going to end well.

Still, I felt so much curiosity about him, so much attraction, how could I walk away? Discombobulated, I left my red scarf on the seat as I disembarked in downtown LA. The next day he emailed me: "It's the morning after. I'm canceling my Match.com account. I'm calling all the women I'm dating and telling them I'm no longer available. More to come."

My first thought was, *My God, how many women are you dating?*

Later, on the phone, he said he felt uncomfortable with my seeing other men. "Would you stop dating other people?"

Flattered by his enthusiasm, I said yes. I was also happy to have an excuse to cancel a date I had the next day. I really wasn't interested in the kinetic psychologist who dominated our conversations after his day of listening to others.

But after I hung up with Jonathan, I felt uneasy acquiescing to the demands of a man I barely knew.

"Insisting on exclusivity after one date?" Neville asked, incredulously.

"I know. I feel like a fool. You give a controlling man an inch..."

"And he'll take a mile."

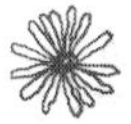

"So now we're exclusive!" Jonathan marveled on the phone the next day. "But I don't know if I can conquer you."

"What? We've gone from exclusivity to conquest?"

"That's not what I mean. It's like you're so independent, I don't know if I can reel you in."

That remark didn't sit well with me, either. Still, I felt invested in Jonathan. He was smart, professionally accomplished, available, and interested in me—a rare combination. At age forty-seven, I was hungry for connection, especially as my romantic choices dwindled.

I agreed to a rendezvous again in two weeks. I'd take the evening train, this time all the way south to San Diego. He'd pick me up at the Del Mar station. Then, I'd return to LA Sunday afternoon.

Staying at a man's house on a second date seemed unwise, to put it mildly. But I'd decided that I needed to take more risks if I was ever going to get married. My friends accused me of "playing it safe." I wanted to prove to myself and to them that they were wrong.

At the train station, our hug was less awkward, more lingering. I felt thrilled as we sped through the night. What an adventure. Then I noticed the lights of the city growing farther apart. I had lived in San Diego for a decade, but we were driving into unfamiliar territory—flat, desert land, far from my former sun-dappled home near the beach.

"You drove quite a ways to pick me up," I remarked, hoping to break the silence.

"Yeah, but it's all freeway."

Yes, we were driving very fast, seemingly away from all signs of civilization.

"Well, hopefully, you didn't have to work too late," I continued.

"No, I choose my own hours. I come and go as I please."

Like a bat in the night.

His silence began to feel ominous. And his free-agent status didn't help. I realized I didn't know where I was, where I was going—and with a man I didn't really know.

After forty-five minutes, Jonathan pulled up to a modest, single-level house at the end of a cul-de-sac dotted with identical homes. The grass in the front yard had long since died; all that remained was flat, dried earth.

Inside, I couldn't detect a single sign of a woman. There were no knickknacks artfully placed. Not a splash of bright color. No throw pillows tucked in the corners of the couch.

"I wanted to show off my house," Jonathan said proudly. "That's why I insisted you visit me." He waved his hand around the spare living room.

The front lawn looked like some place where bodies were buried, and the minimal decor made the house resemble the digs of a drifter. It certainly didn't feel like the home of a father who hosted two young sons every other weekend. For a moment, I thought, *I've got to get out of here. Maybe I should call a taxi—if there's even one available a million miles from nowhere.* But I had written my glowing script in my mind. We would fall in love and quickly. Aborting the weekend before it had begun did not fit my plotline.

Jonathan rolled my overnight bag into his sons' bedroom. "You'll be sleeping here *tonight*," he said, as if the next night would be a different story.

On the wall facing the bed, he'd hung a photo of himself. He was about twenty-one, shirtless and tan, his pixie mouth spread in a wide grin. Now his eyes were smaller, his skin pasty, his shoulders rounded. I suspected he'd hung the photo there expressly for my visit. Or perhaps it was a permanent fixture.

Judging by the number of women he was dating when we met, the photo might have contributed to a well-worn routine for wooing potential paramours.

He insisted that we sit cross-legged facing each other on his living room carpet. "I want to teach you Tantric breathing," he said. "Look me in the eye. Follow my inhales and exhales." He'd mentioned his desire to give me Tantric lessons in an earlier email, so I knew what this breathing was meant to be: a prelude to Tantric sex.

My heart sank. *Good God, I found another one.*

"Mmmmm," I said after ten minutes, my polite way of indicating I'd had enough.

"I like it when you say, 'Mmmmm,'" Jonathan said, pressing his forehead against mine.

We kissed, and our physical chemistry temporarily obscured my doubts.

When he started to take off my blouse, though, I pulled away. "I think it's a little too soon for this."

"We're just getting to know each other," he insisted.

"A little too quickly for my tastes," I said, as I rebuttoned my blouse.

"So what do you want me to do?"

"Talk and hold my hand, something like that," I said taking his hand in mine.

He pulled away and glared at me. "No, I think it's time for bed."

We retired to our respective bedrooms. As he shut his door, I shut mine, then stretched out on his son's narrow bottom bunk. Through the bottom sheet, I could feel the mattress had been covered in plastic. *I'm such a frickin' idiot,* I scolded myself. *Here I am in some strange man's home. No one knows where I am. I don't even know where I am.*

I decided to steal outside to check the house number and street name. That way I could call Neville and let him know my whereabouts in case I went missing. I tiptoed down the driveway, surrounded by the grassless yard. I could barely make out the numbers painted on the curb—*1 7 0 9*. I whispered the number over and over. In my heightened state of anxiety, I doubted I could remember even four digits.

I padded down the sidewalk, searching for a street sign. A dog barked a few houses down, violently scratching on the windowpane as I passed. After a block, there still was no sign. Dogs howled in the distance. Or maybe they were coyotes. I wasn't sure. It probably wasn't wise to keep walking in a strange, nearly pitch-black neighborhood. My footwear—rubber flip-flops—was definitely not designed for fleeing wild dogs. Some mail on the kitchen table will indicate the address, I assured myself.

As I stole up the driveway to Jonathan's door, I saw his form pressed against the living room window. Had he been watching me the whole time? I panicked.

"What are you doing?" he demanded.

"Oh, just taking an evening stroll," I said, my words sounding calmer than I felt.

"Why didn't you ask me to go with you?"

"I thought you'd already be asleep. I didn't want to bother you."

"Maybe I should put a leash on you, so you don't go wandering off by yourself."

Now I have to worry about being held captive? I wondered. *Should I bolt for it while I have a chance?*

"The night air is so refreshing," I said, ignoring his comment. "But I'm ready for bed now. Sleep well." With that, I made a beeline for the bunk room.

I locked the door as quietly as I could, then shoved his son's desk chair under the door handle for added protection. I lay on the bunk. My ears were ringing, and my T-shirt was soaked with sweat. I wanted to take off all my clothes and climb under the cool sheets. But that felt way too vulnerable. I kicked off my flip-flops and settled on top of the covers. With all my clothes on, I was ready to escape if need be. Only after a prolonged meditation could I coax myself to sleep.

On Saturday morning, I peeked out the bedroom window. San Diego's signature clean air, bright sun, and turquoise sky beckoned. Surely nothing untoward could happen on such a day. I pressed my ear against the bedroom door. The coast was clear. But, as I opened it, I heard a voice from the other side of the house. "I've been waiting for you," Jonathan announced.

I jumped. Maybe he had the leash he'd spoken of last night. "Good morning," I called out, trying to hide my panic.

"Your breakfast is ready."

I quickly peed and joined him in the dinette. He set down a mug of coffee, toast, and a jar of Welch's grape jam.

"I thought we might go to my favorite park."

"Sounds fun," I said, although anything that got me out of this tiny, dirt-lawned house sounded like a great idea. "I'll put on some boots and cargo shorts." I scarfed down the toast and headed back to the bunk room to slip on my outfit, which included a tank top. I still had high hopes for the weekend. Maybe we'd just gotten off to a bad start.

We drove in silence. I looked out the window to get my bearings. Nothing looked familiar from my days of living in San Diego.

Suddenly, Jonathan pulled over.

Oh, God, now what?

"What would you think of Sufi dancing instead?"

As an avid dancer, in ballet, tap, and modern, I was up for sacred Middle Eastern dance. Still, I was surprised by the change of plans. Maybe it was for the best, though. Upon reflection, I realized a walk in the park might involve significant time alone in the woods with Jonathan. Definitely not a smart plan.

When we arrived at the community room of a Unitarian church, I noted the ratio of women to men. It was 5:1, a common phenomenon I'd experienced in my own pursuit of new age activities. Even worse, the women were dressed in see-through harem pants and colorful peasant skirts. A diamond stud gleamed in one woman's navel. In the restroom, a lady stood at the mirror combing her waist-length red hair.

"Do you think I'm dressed appropriately?" I asked the woman, feeling decidedly unfeminine in my hiking gear.

"I'm a nudist," she said. "I never worry about dress codes."

The facilitator gave each of us a handful of tiny heart-shaped stickers. Jonathan covered my bare left shoulder with a cascade of hearts. I stuck one on his "third eye" in the middle of his forehead.

In the first dance, the leader directed us to form our arms in a big circle above our heads. "I am the sun," we sang. Slowly, we swung our arms down to the floor. "I am the light." I tried not to laugh. Jonathan was obviously taking this movement very seriously, as was the accompanist, a slight, effeminate man dressed in all white who played a portable keyboard.

The leader instructed us to form into twosomes. Jonathan pulled me close, and I felt a rush of comfort in his arms. After a few minutes we had to switch partners. He moved on to the nudist with the long hair and I to a short, forty-something man wearing an expression of perpetual surprise. We rotated partners again and again, until we'd danced with everyone in the room.

"So, what did you think?" he asked as we drove back to his house, the heart sticker still stuck in the center of his forehead.

"I have to admit, I feel a lot of warmth and affection, almost like I'm high." What I didn't say was that I couldn't recognize my own scent because the smell of twenty-five dance partners stuck to me.

"That's what happens when you come in contact with so many open-hearted people," he explained.

It was dinnertime, but Jonathan made no mention of restaurant reservations or a home-cooked meal. I suspected he had another plan, one which featured me as the main course. The Sufi dancing had been our foreplay.

We started to make out on the couch. As we kissed, he said, "Say 'I love you, Jonathan.'"

"What? I don't even know you!"

"That's okay. You don't have to mean it. Just say the words. It's no big deal."

"Okay," I said to shut him up. "I love you, Jonathan."

"That wasn't so bad, was it?"

Actually, it *was* pretty bad. I felt like a call girl hired to act out a fantasy. My real feelings were of no interest.

"And it would be really great if you shaved off your muff."

"What?"

"Then I could kiss you down there."

"How do you even know if I've shaved or not?"

"I suspect you haven't."

I scooted to the far end of the couch and folded my arms across my chest. "You want to tell me what to say and how to look?"

Jonathan got up and slowly tucked his shirt into his pants. He walked to his bedroom and closed the door behind him as if I weren't even there.

In a matter of sixty seconds, he'd pushed all my buttons: *You're invisible. You're not good enough as is. And, if you don't do what I want, I'll abandon you.*

I was furious and, I suddenly realized, starving. I scrounged through his refrigerator, but all I found was a half-drunk McDonald's milkshake and baloney, both of dubious freshness.

Even from the kitchen, I could hear him snoring loudly. He was definitely down for the count. I tiptoed to his bedroom and slowly opened his door. He lay spread-eagled on his California king, a bed definitely designed for company. A mouth guard pulled his pixie mouth into a snarl. Did he grind his teeth, too?

I quietly shut the door. Maybe I'll read the *LA Times* I brought—do something normal in this sea of abnormality. Instead, I decided to take advantage of my first moment of freedom. I could snoop around his house without getting caught, unless he woke up.

I studied the living room. Framed documents hung on every wall. They looked like diplomas of some sort. When I stepped closer, I saw they were certificates of completion for workshops, with names like *Mastering the Art of Attracting, Dating, and Seducing Women* and *Updates for Innovative Relationship Creation*. At the bottom of one certificate, it read: "Jonathan Nelson has completed 36 hours in *Loving Choices, Section II*." I recalled our earlier conversation on ICQ when he wrote "God assigned me the role of Senator of the Spiritual Realm to teach people how to love." Apparently, he needed a little help in that capacity.

Next to the certificates hung framed, handwritten letters. I moved closer to read one:

Dear Princess:

I feel your presence now. I'll wait until the time is right. And then I'll love you with all my might.

Love,
Jonathan

I suspected that one of the relationship seminars had assigned this visualization exercise to help participants attract their soulmate. Jonathan had told me he maintained an Excel spreadsheet where he'd rate prospective mates on two hundred qualities. He measured each trait—looks, prowess in bed, punctuality, and so on—on a 0–5 scale, from "poor" to "excellent." A certain composite score qualified a woman as an ideal mate—no doubt, the woman he addressed as "Dear Princess" in the framed letter. This weekend he was auditioning me for that role.

I remembered what Jonathan said he had learned during his near-death experience: to plug into the divine, not a person, as his primary source of power. Apparently, that lesson had fallen on deaf ears.

In the midst of the letters and diplomas, there were no photos of his parents, his sons, or even a friend. I returned to the bunk room to study the one and only photo in the house, the one of Jonathan tanned, toned, shirtless, and young. His image reminded me of the outdated photos men posted on their Match.com profiles.

I locked the door behind me and called Neville. Thank God there was a phone on his son's desk. "He fell asleep at 8 p.m.," I whispered. "We never had dinner!"

"Keep in mind," he pointed out, "men are on their best behavior when they first start dating a woman."

"My God, just think of what he's like when he's behaving badly! Listen, I better get off before he wakes up and hears us talking."

I relied on another long meditation to fall asleep.

When I woke the next morning, the house was eerily silent and cold. Jonathan must have turned up the air-conditioning. I quickly got dressed without showering. I didn't want any surprise visitors in the bathroom. I found him at the kitchen table, eating a bowl of dry Cocoa Puffs.

"Out of milk?" I said, hoping to break the ice.

"I felt distant from you when you didn't sleep with me," he said, ignoring my question. He set out a second bowl of milk-less cereal and a mug of coffee for me. I started munching the brown orbs, trying to wash them down with the coffee.

Really? I thought. *If intimacy was what you were after, whatever happened to engaging conversation over an evening meal? Or did you miss that class?*

"I checked, and there's a train leaving in an hour."

Thank God. The weekend was over. "Okay, I'll go get my stuff." I wanted to move fast, lest he change his mind.

He rolled my suitcase out past his dirt lawn, now slightly muddy from the night fog. The warm sun felt good on my skin after the overly air-conditioned house. I chatted away on the trip to the station, trying to alleviate the tension in the air. But he said nothing except, "You're in your head, not your heart."

Knowing I'd never see him again, I spoke my mind for the first time. "That's a strange comment coming from a software engineer who must be in his head forty, fifty hours a week . . . not to mention someone who so carefully orchestrated this weekend with only one end in mind."

Jonathan said nothing. Then he started talking, but so quietly I couldn't make out what he was saying. He glanced at the sky. He seemed to be having a conversation with a flock of ravens flying overhead.

"So, what do the crows have to say today?" I asked, trying to make a joke.

When he didn't respond, I realized he really *was* talking to the birds. My breath quickened. His mental state now in question, I wondered if he was driving me to the train station after all.

"You're perfect," he said, this time speaking to me, not the crows. "But you're going to dump me."

He talked as if we were ending a long association, instead of one spanning only two dates.

"I don't think I'll ever find my princess," he continued after a long pause.

"Why do you say that?"

"I'm too different."

"Different" wasn't the right word. "Dysfunctional" was more like it. Not that I was one to talk. Taking a train to the-middle-of-God-knows-where to spend a weekend with a guy I hardly knew—well, that wasn't exactly sane either. I was trying so hard to mate, I'd lost my marbles.

He pulled into the parking lot of the Del Mar train station. After unloading my suitcase from his trunk, he turned to me with tears in his eyes. "This is goodbye."

I said nothing, just turned and walked quickly to the train tracks, the wheels of my suitcase rattling loudly over the platform's wooden slats.

As the train sped north toward LA, I watched the ocean crashing to my left. The more distance between me and Jonathan, the more relief I felt. I called Neville on the train pay phone to relay the saga.

"You're lucky you escaped with your life," he said.

Chapter 29

A MAN NAMED MELANIE

After my disastrous liaison with Jonathan, I hibernated for a while. But with my supposed expiration of desirability just a few years away, I felt compelled to shop before the "store closed." So when a friend offered to set me up on a blind date with Mel in September 2000, I agreed.

In the crowded foyer of a macrobiotic restaurant, Mel appeared a few minutes late. Tall and loose-limbed, he bore the accoutrements of a twenty-first-century man—black clogs, linen clam diggers, a bright yellow Live Strong rubber wristband, and a tiny hoop in his left ear. But his face—pale and earnest—came from another century.

He told me that he was a divorced father of a seven-year-old son and owned a company that designed signage for architects. He seemed serious, not the playful, lighthearted sort that typically appealed to me. Even our meal at the restaurant he'd selected seemed serious—a mound of yam in an earthen bowl.

When we said goodbye, he gazed at me with celadon eyes and wrapped his long, graceful fingers around mine. I looked down, suddenly shy. I noticed he'd shaved his calves.

On our second date, Mel and I retreated to the atrium bar of the Ritz-Carlton in downtown LA. We'd ditched a cacophonous dance performance in favor of a quieter, more intimate setting.

"I have something I need to tell you," he announced, before we'd even ordered drinks. Mel considered me a moment, then popped a handful of peanuts in his mouth. After he finished chewing, he said, "I like to cross-dress." His confession came without a trace of apology, just an attitude: *This is who I am. Take it or leave it.*

Momentarily speechless, I remembered his apartment overlooked Ross Dress for Less, one of LA's less appealing discount stores.

"What are you doing, shopping at Cross-dress for Less?" I joked.

He laughed, then drew my hand along the length of his thigh. Under his khakis, I felt the buckle of a garter and the smoothness of a silk stocking.

"My God, *now*?" I whispered. We were alone, waiting for a server who never came.

I felt flattered that he'd disclosed such a private matter and was drawn closer by our shared secret. Only later did worry set in: Maybe he's gay. Maybe he wants to become a woman. Maybe he's hiding something else.

Suddenly, I remembered his shaved legs. He was an avid cyclist, he had told me on our first date. Maybe that's what cyclists do, I thought at the time. Now I realized, maybe that's what cross-dressers do.

Yearning to decipher Mel's hidden side, I buried myself in the local library, poring through academic journals like *Archives of Sexual Behavior* and *Sex Roles: A Journal of Research*. To my relief, I learned that most cross-dressers—87 percent, according to one survey—describe themselves as heterosexuals. The high probability that Mel was straight reassured me.

However unusual Mel's proclivities, I really liked the guy. He possessed some of the qualities of my ideal mate: well-mannered, intelligent, and capable of reciprocal conversation. I decided to see where the relationship would take us.

For the time being, that meant the mall. Although he'd shopped for women's clothing for several years, he had never shopped with a partner. His wife and his past several girlfriends had shown no interest.

Late on a Tuesday, when Macy's was nearly deserted, we snuck him into the fitting room of the women's clothing department. I modeled his first selection, a black spandex skirt with plastic triangles dangling at the hem. He liked the look, so I took it off for him to try on. As he dropped his jeans, I was astounded by what I saw: a 6'1" man in coral bikini panties edged in lace.

"Well, I can see you've been shopping already," I said, trying to hide my shock.

"Do you like?" he asked, jutting one hip to the side in a model's pose. "I got them at the big girls' store."

"Maybe you ought to take *me* shopping," I said, quickly climbing back into my jeans. I didn't want him to get too good a look at what *I* was wearing: Hanes three-in-a-pack white briefs printed with tiny pink poodles.

To complement the skirt, Mel had selected a fitted taupe blouse, high enough at the neck to hide his chest hair and tailored to show off his waist, which was slim from daily cycling.

"Perfect! You've got a great eye."

Just then the salesclerk stepped toward us on the other side of the curtain. Mel, now dressed from head to toe as a woman, opened his mouth wide in terror. I pressed my index finger to my lips, signaling him to keep quiet.

"How're ya doin' in there?" the clerk asked.

"Just fine," I replied curtly. I didn't want her asking any questions.

After the clerk left, Mel regained his composure and studied his reflection in the mirror. Apparently liking what he saw, he reached into his pocket, then lay four twenties across my palm. "You buy the skirt and blouse," he instructed, folding my fingers across the bills.

He stood ten feet away from the checkout counter. We shot each other a look while I paid the bill.

We took the escalator to the first floor. As we strolled down the aisle separating the menswear and cosmetics departments, Mel stopped me. "Look to your left," he directed.

There stretched a sea of black and brown suits, stacks of white button-down shirts, and turnstiles of monochromatic ties.

"Now look to your right."

Crystal perfume bottles gleamed on gold trays. Pink and red lipstick lined brightly lit display cases. A Chanel salesclerk looked at me expectantly, a fan-shaped makeup brush poised to powder my cheeks.

Mel threw up his hands in despair. "Now tell me, who would *you* rather be?"

"You're right," I said. "It *is* more fun to be a girl, at least at Macy's."

Back at my condo, Mel slowly became "Melanie." He put on his new skirt and blouse, then slipped on a pair of fishnet stockings. He held still while I lined his eyes and brushed mascara on his lashes. Demonstrating a graphic designer's steady hand, he painted his lips and applied eye shadow.

To add to the drama, I unearthed a Tina Turner–style shag wig that I'd worn one Halloween.

"Perfect," he said.

I struggled to collect his hair under the wig, yanking it down to hide his sideburns. Then I stepped back to study my handiwork. I'd been so consumed with the details, I wasn't prepared for the final result. Melanie looked like a middle-aged matron who'd emerged from her Buick to get her nails done.

"Oh my God," she said, gazing at herself in the mirror. "I look like my older sister. I can't stand her!"

"That shows how convincing you are."

By this time, it was midnight—time to go. We both had to get up early for work. She took off her newly purchased clothes and grew somber.

"We're going to have so much fun unwrapping Melanie," I said. "Speaking of which, be careful taking off your fishnets or they'll run. Sit on the bed. I'll demonstrate."

She lifted one leg, then the other, as I slowly slipped them off. We weren't focused on each other so much as on Melanie—taking care of her like a newly arrived guest.

Now back to Mel, he washed off his makeup and lovingly folded the skirt and blouse in the tissue paper they had been wrapped in. Then he started to cry. I sensed he was stuffing Melanie back out of sight, along with everything else he'd been hiding for years.

"We'll be seeing more of her," I said, trying to comfort him. "Don't you worry." I put the wig back in its box. "Here, take it. I think Melanie likes it." I retrieved a black velvet clutch from a drawer. "Take this, too. It'll make the outfit."

Mel left, with the wig box and clutch tucked under one arm and his Macy's bag slung over the other.

I sat on the edge of the bed staring straight ahead. Part of me felt a giddy guilt, as if Mel and I were seven and we'd just stolen into my mother's closet. We'd tried on her high heels and lipstick without getting caught. But we weren't seven. We were forty-seven. I'd always prided myself at weathering men's idiosyncrasies. This time, though, I'd gotten in over my head.

Busy running his business and raising his son, Mel didn't have much time to date, at least not for the next few weeks. Instead, we talked on the phone, sometimes for two hours at a stretch, sharing intimacies we might have hesitated to disclose so soon in person.

"I've never been married," I said sheepishly. "I've never been close to getting married."

Mel mirrored my honesty. "I'm taking three antidepressants a day, shelling out $200 to my pharmacist every month. I married my wife at twenty-eight, not because I loved her or shared anything in common with her, but because she was so cheerful. I hoped she'd take away my depression."

Viewing a woman this way felt ominous. Was I slated to become another tablet to add to his three-pill regimen? But men had waved so many red flags at me, I'd gotten expert at ignoring them.

Sensing my disquiet, Mel drew me back in. "You're one of the most engaging people I've met in a long time," he whispered. "I'm fully present with you. You're an adult."

I found this last comment jarring. Unlike me, he had met all the entrance requirements of adulthood—marriage, child, and business ownership. In my eyes, *he* was the grownup. In fact, I felt slightly embarrassed talking to a grownup when I didn't feel like one.

We continued to date, developing a habit of shaking hands in a long, lingering grasp when we said goodbye. It was almost sexier than a kiss—but not quite. After two months, I believed it was time to get physical.

"Come on over Saturday night," I told him on the phone. "Let me make you dinner."

Mel pulled up late Saturday afternoon in his silver Saturn station wagon. "I didn't wash my car," he said. "I didn't fall into that date preparation frenzy."

I, on the other hand, had spent the whole week crafting the dinner menu and shopping for lingerie, which I carefully laid out on my bed, hoping the evening would end there.

Immediately, I put Mel to work. He proved expert with a paring knife, carefully chopping scallions and carrots in even slivers for our dinner salad. Then he lit the votive candles with a flourish. I studied his hands. His fingers were slender and obviously coordinated.

We sat down to eat our artichoke pasta and Caesar salad. Mel kept his left hand in his lap as he ate. After we finished, he leaned over and kissed me. I quickly climbed in his lap, then pulled him under the dining room table to make out. Every so often, we knelt at the table's edge to take a swig of wine.

I had wanted to feel the underside of his long, pale arms, taut from cycling. They were just as soft and creamy and hairless as I had hoped. And the physical chemistry I had yearned for was there, too.

After we banged our heads a few times on the legs of the dining room table, Mel said, "Maybe a more comfortable place is in order."

While rolling around under the dining room table fit the theme of our dates—always breaking the mold—I agreed that climbing into my double bed might be better. But first I excused myself to the bathroom to don my new lacy camisole and panties.

I'd like to say we then made wild, passionate love. But Mel performed in bed the same way he'd sliced the scallions for our dinner salad—carefully, thoroughly, precisely. He acted like this was the way a man is supposed to behave the first time in bed with a lady.

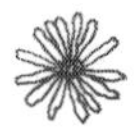

The following week, Mel decided it was *his* turn to plan our date. He wanted to take his freshly assembled outfit—the fitted taupe blouse and black skirt with plastic dangles—for a test drive. During an internet search, he'd learned that a local gay restaurant, the Venture Inn, reserved a corner table for cross-dressers every Saturday night. He showed me a photo on the inn's website—a raucous table of eight held up their wineglasses in a toast.

"Would you escort Melanie to her debut dinner?" he asked. "From the picture, it looks as if wives and girlfriends join, too."

"How can I turn down a date at the Venture Inn?" I joked, wondering what I was getting myself into.

It took us two hours to transform Mel into Melanie. I'd never acknowledged what a woman goes through to become socially presentable. From blow-dry, mascara, and nail polish to pumps, pantyhose, and pendant necklace, I counted two dozen steps. But the effort was worth it. Mel loved being the focus of my pampering. And I relished my first experience primping a man.

Melanie teetered down the back stairs of my Santa Monica condo and stood next to the passenger door of my car.

"Get in," I said as I climbed into the driver's seat.

She looked at me expectantly. I realized she was waiting for me to be the "gentleman." I unhooked my seatbelt, got out, and circled the car to the passenger side.

"Here you go, miss," I said, opening her door. Before I shut it, I tucked her skirt safely inside.

Playing "the man," I felt my sense of agency grow. *I* was the master of this ship. Emboldened, I pulled onto the highway.

After a few blocks, Melanie giggled. "Oh, oh, I forgot something."

"What? Do you want to go back?" I said, pulling over.

"I left the restaurant address at home."

Exasperated, I popped open my cell to call the Venture Inn. "Could you give me directions from the 101?" I asked the host. "And when do . . ." I hesitated. "When do the cross-dressers meet?"

He gave me expert directions, then added, "The CDs congregate at the entrance around 7 p.m."

"We still have time to convene with the other CDs," I told Melanie after I hung up. "That's how the host described the cross-dressers."

"Good to know the lingo," she said wryly.

True to the host's word, our companions for the evening awaited on the sidewalk. "Amy" and "Sharon," "Paula" and "Amanda" introduced themselves, as they wobbled on stilettos. They held up their pocketbooks for protection as teenage boys careened by on skateboards.

They'd carpooled from Lydia's, a service that specialized in transforming men into women prior to a night on the town.

I scanned the group for the "real" women. Apparently, the other females had begged off, so I was on my own. Now, instead of ushering just one CD to dinner, I was shepherding five. As I led the pack into the restaurant, I hoped I was up to the task.

The maître d' led us to a large round table in a dark corner. Men at the bar stared at the "women" as they paraded by. The gay community accepted CDs, I suspected, but with clear limits—as long as they showed up just one night a week and stayed in their relegated section.

Sharon, a 250-pound tour bus driver, with red press-on nails and a giant rhinestone ring, ordered a one-pound tenderloin steak. Amy, a business consultant from Houston on a four-month assignment in LA, ordered a baked potato with "everything on it." Paula—Paul in his real life as a creative director at an insurance agency—proceeded to dominate the conversation. There was no denying I was in the company of men.

As the evening wore on, some of the CDs disclosed details of their cross-dressing. Sharon had become a shopaholic, picking up women's clothes at swap meets and thrift stores until her purchases had taken over the closet she shared with her wife.

"I'm dieting so I can fit into this gorgeous tennis dress I spotted window shopping," Sharon shared. "At least I think that's what it is. What's the difference between a tennis dress and a cheerleading outfit?"

"Well, both are mid-thigh," I explained, "but a tennis dress is often white or pastel, while a cheerleading outfit is usually in bright school colors."

Sharon bowed her head in gratitude for this clarification.

When I complimented Amy on her scarf, she seemed genuinely pleased. It hid her Adam's apple, another part of the male anatomy that needed obscuring. "I've never told anyone about dressing like this, least of all my wife," she told me. I felt privileged to be hearing secrets these CDs rarely shared with anyone.

The "gals" felt no qualms about joining me in the ladies' room. Nor did I. But I stifled a giggle when I heard them struggling with their pantyhose in the stalls next to mine, falling into the partition separating our toilets when they lost their balance.

Later, as they leaned into the mirror to reapply their lipstick, most overshot their lip line. They lacked the practiced hand of most women. I ducked out without talking to them. I had enough on my hands just dealing with Melanie.

Back at the table, she sat quietly to my left, my velvet clutch perched demurely in her lap. Occasionally, she fingered the pendant necklace we'd made for the occasion at a local bead shop. Unlike Mel, who rarely smiled, Melanie smiled almost constantly. I squeezed her knee. This outing was her first appearance in public as a woman. I didn't want to underestimate the magnitude of the occasion.

As for me, I loved my ringside seat in this exotic theater with its awkward logistics and brave breaches of convention. When the check came, I grabbed it out of Melanie's hand. We drove home in silence. What we'd each experienced was too complex to share at the time.

The next day, I told my therapist, Joyce, about the new guy I was dating. As our session ended, she advised, "Remember, you have to sacrifice a piece of the 'me' to make a 'we.'"

I didn't get a chance to ask her, "So what happens when the 'we' is actually three?" Welcoming a third party was supposed to be my way of capturing Mel's heart when I suspected it was doing the opposite—writing myself out of the script.

From Mel's perspective, dinner at the Venture Inn had served as his coming-out party. On Monday, he booked appointments to get his hair streaked blond and his other ear pierced with a sapphire stud. On his lunch hour, he snapped up the kimono top embroidered with birds that he'd been eyeing at a local Japanese gift shop.

And he commissioned me to order T-strap heels on Zappos, which I'd recommended as a more comfortable alternative to pumps.

"They grip the foot," I explained, "making them easier to walk in, especially for someone new to such footwear."

"My God, there are 548 T-straps to choose from," he lamented, as we scrolled through page after page of shoes. "How can I possibly decide?"

"Let's go with a Sesto Meucci. That's always worked for me. And I suggest a size 12."

"The biggest size?" he asked in mock offense.

"That would be a 'yes,' but you'll fill them well." I hoped I was right. I didn't want to disappoint Mel as I guided his transformation.

Soon after, he joined Shifting Gears, a lesbian cycling club whose members bicycled in the Santa Monica mountains every Sunday morning. Taken aback by his deep voice on the phone, the leader was even more surprised when Mel showed up as Melanie for the first ride. She was dressed in full makeup, the Tina Turner wig, and lime-green spandex. Giggling after this first ride with the club, Mel said, "Now that I'm a member, they'll probably change the club's name to Shiftless Queers!"

While the leader of Shifting Gears balked at Melanie, I found myself energized in her company—far more than in Mel's. Melanie was lighthearted, almost giddy, not dour like Mel.

Even better, there was no sense of "doing" the relationship. With Mel, I always felt as if he was doing what a guy is supposed to do: he paid the right compliments, comported himself politely, brought over just the right gift, and made love like a proper gentleman.

With Melanie, we enjoyed each other's company with no prewritten script. Besides, Melanie was our shared project, something we could work on together.

Still, there were troubling signs. In a moment of passion, when I pushed Mel up against the broom closet door with a loud thud, he said, "I love it when you're strong like that, when you're the man."

I felt like saying, *Hey, buddy, remember, I'm* not *the guy.*

Later, perplexed by a new cell phone, I solicited his help. He acted offended. I suspected he bridled at my casting us in stereotypical gender roles—the IT-clueless woman asking the technologically savvy man to rescue her. I called tech support in Mumbai.

And while I bent over backward to accommodate Melanie, Mel did not reciprocate. He grudgingly agreed to join me at a church service led by my favorite monk. But afterward, he disparaged the sermon. He even admitted he considered breaking up with me. How could he marry a woman who believed in all that? That hurt. I felt that my open-mindedness about Melanie should have entitled me to his acceptance of my spiritual pursuit. Apparently not.

Valentine's Day was fast approaching, and with it all the pressures as to how to celebrate, what gift to buy, whether to sign the card "Fondly," "Affectionately," or with the "*L* word." Equally stressful was wondering who would show up at my door come February 14—Mel or Melanie. I suspected Melanie would like to be acknowledged; after all, a lot of women cherish Valentine's Day. I decided to ask Melanie to be my date.

But when Melanie returned from a Sunday morning bike ride, she seemed uncharacteristically glum.

"What's wrong?"

"Shifting Gears kicked me out of the club."

"Oh, no! Why?"

"They said I didn't fit their member profile."

"I'm so sorry." I paused. "*I'd* like to include Melanie, in something else that is."

"What do you mean?"

"Would she like to celebrate Valentine's Day?"

Melanie stared at me, incredulous. "You'd actually do that for me?"

"Of course," I said, suddenly realizing what I'd gotten myself into.

That night I pondered the prospect of buying a Valentine's Day gift for a boyfriend-turned-girlfriend. I couldn't rely on Victoria's Secret. The store designed lingerie for women—not a 6'1" man with biceps and buns muscled from speed cycling.

Later, while walking from yoga class to my favorite dress shop in Venice, I noticed a store I'd never seen before called Hidden Vestments. It featured an androgynous mannequin in the window sporting a red lace-up bustier, garters and black fishnets. A sign read: WHY CAN'T MEN DRESS IN LACE IF WOMEN WEAR TROUSERS? Underneath, in smaller type, it said: CUSTOM LINGERIE AND GOWNS FOR BOTH. BY APPOINTMENT ONLY.

I tried the door, but true to the sign, the shop was locked. I was confused. This area was the main drag of Venice, not a side street in West Hollywood's "Boy's Town." Then I recalled my earlier research in *Sex Roles: A Journal of Research*. Six percent of Americans cross-dress. The practice was more common than I'd initially imagined. I jotted down the phone number, too chicken to dial it right away.

The next day, I marshaled my courage. The person who answered identified herself, but I couldn't quite catch her name.

"Fran?" I repeated to see if I had it right.

"No, *Fram*," she said, sounding irritated.

Maybe it was a combination of "Fran" and "Sam." Her voice could have gone either way. I suspected that, like Mel and Melanie, she straddled the sexes. I scheduled an appointment for the next weekend.

On Saturday, a few minutes before 10 a.m., I knocked on the door of Hidden Vestments. The door buzzed open. I felt like I was entering a diamond shop on Rodeo Drive, the lock on the door electronically released only if the patron looked presentable or had an appointment.

Inside, the shop was nearly dark. I stood for a moment, waiting for my eyes to adjust from the bright seaside sun. When I could make out my surroundings, I thought I'd made a mistake. Instead of a lingerie shop, it looked like an intimate Catholic chapel.

In the entryway, vintage prayer cards hung on the wall, each lit underneath by a single votive candle. Saints in elaborately brocaded vestments—purple, red, and gold—stared out at me, some with halos, others making the sign of the Benediction. Only one prayer card revealed that I was in the right place. It featured a buff, blond man in an aqua teddy and boxer shorts, both trimmed in lace.

Suddenly a tall shadow appeared in the gloom. "Hi, I'm Fram."

She reminded me of the "women" Melanie and I had dined with at the Venture Inn, with fingernails a little too long and makeup a little too thick. We shook hands.

"I first realized the need for men's lingerie while running a bridal shop," she began, trying to put me at ease. "I caught men copping a feel of the lace on wedding gowns. And, increasingly, couples requested matching wedding-night underwear. Then it hit me. Here was this untapped market—creating underthings for men. I mean, the saints wore embroidery and satin." She gestured toward the prayer cards in the foyer. "Why can't we all?"

Fram ushered me to an armchair and handed me a catalog. The first page featured a floral tank-and-brief set billed as "the perfect counterpoint to your wool pinstripes" and a $200 midriff-baring vest-and-boxer set. The shorts had a strip of rabbit fur at the waistband.

"Saints wore *this*?" I asked, looking up from the catalog.

"Before the eighteenth century, elegant people of *both* sexes wore scent, rouge, and high heels, along with lace and brocade . . . even the saints."

"Not now, though."

"Back then, people didn't worry about the sexuality of men in lace, spangles, and embroidery. But beginning in the late seventeenth century, the elegant clothing of men and women came to be increasingly divided."

Her well-rehearsed sales pitch assuaged my doubts. Mel had simply been born in the wrong century.

Fram flipped the pages of the catalog and stopped at a pink net thong edged in black ruffles. "This item has been quite popular lately." Whispering, she added, "It's expandable to accommodate any basket."

I decided on the thong and, in a nod to Mel's passion for cycling, a black "cabaret set" of bicycle pants and lace-up bustier from the shop's most expensive collection, "Midnight."

I gave Fram the measurements that I had surreptitiously taken while Mel slept. His bed-time regime of three antidepressants knocked him out cold, allowing me—undetected—to wrap my tape measure around his waist and chest.

"Thank you for such specific measurements. Most women just approximate. I'll have my seamstress sew the items by February 13." I paid and she showed me to the door.

I emerged onto the sidewalk, squinting in the bright sun. The oddness of Hidden Vestments, like the Venture Inn, captivated me. Then Mel called, as if tuned into my intense focus on his desires.

"Could you choose a restaurant for Valentine's Day and make reservations?" he asked, breathlessly on his cell phone. He was fighting traffic on the way to an appointment with his most difficult client, one of the top architectural firms in the city.

By now, I'd tacitly agreed to play the man's role as Mel increasingly played the woman's role. I was arranging Valentine's Day, a holiday usually orchestrated by a man. I made reservations at Pradeep's, an Indian restaurant with well-spaced tables so we could enjoy some privacy.

A week later, I picked up the custom-sewn thong, bustier, and bicycle pants at Hidden Vestments. I carefully wrapped each gift in sparkly lavender tissue and tied it with pink foil ribbon. I knew exactly what kind of frills Melanie would appreciate on Valentine's Day.

For our date, Melanie arrived at my door in full makeup and wearing her new gray silk kimono top, which was embroidered with pastel birds and flowers at the cuffs. She cut a slim silhouette in her black pencil skirt, and her T-strap heels looked feminine in spite of their large size.

"You look fabulous," I said.

"Think so?" she asked, searching my face to see if I meant it.

"Absolutely."

What I didn't say was that the wig, pulled too low on her forehead, gave her a slight Neanderthal look. And her baritone voice didn't help either.

I wore a simple black pantsuit—a nod to my appointed role as the guy—and so as not to outshine Melanie. I wanted her to claim center stage.

As we navigated the two blocks from my condo to the restaurant, I switched to the street side, as my father had when he walked with me. It was a gentlemanly custom originally designed to protect the lady from mud splattered by horse-drawn carriages. Now the mud was of a different sort. A woman could wear trousers in public, but a man wearing a skirt could lead to bullying or worse. In my appointed role as the man, I felt responsible for Melanie's safety.

When we arrived at Pradeep's, I was surprised to find that the tables had doubled in number to accommodate the Valentine's Day crowd; they were spaced within inches of each other. We sat down and overheard the woman next to us whisper to her date, "Only in LA." I gave Melanie a worried look. Instead of being offended, she smiled, pleased that she'd been noticed.

I marveled at our waitress's composure, too. After a slight double take, she calmly asked, "And what would the young lady like to drink tonight?" Melanie beamed. I could see that comment alone had made her evening.

The guests on either side of us eventually accepted that we were just another couple celebrating Valentine's Day. They nodded admiringly when I opened my gift—a lovely silver bracelet Mel had bought at the mall.

Then, Melanie untied her package. The pink thong came tumbling out, its color practically glowing in the table's candlelight. The couple to our right stared with their mouths open, shocked by what they were seeing.

"I love it!" Melanie exclaimed, quickly slipping it and the other lingerie in her lap. "But you've already given me the ultimate gift."

"Which is?"

"You saw what would make me happy and agreed to it. No one's ever done that for me."

I squeezed her hand, pleased that she felt special, especially on Valentine's Day. Still, I felt unsettled. I could attend to Melanie—dress her, buy her gifts, take her to dinner—but the deeper meaning behind her cross-dressing was something I couldn't comprehend. Her yearning, I suspected, went far beyond a guy who likes to dress like a gal. I felt pressed up against a window I couldn't see through. The mystery disturbed me, but also captivated me. I kept wanting to know what would happen next.

The waitress delivered the dessert menu. We studied the featured heart-shaped ice cream sundae. Melanie closed the menu. "Let's skip dessert," she said. "I want to try on my new outfit!"

Yikes, I thought. Buying the gifts had been challenging, but not as hard as what lay ahead. Melanie would model her lingerie, then want to take them for a test drive. I didn't know if I was up for that. *It's Valentine's Day*, I reminded myself. *You'd better be.*

"Let's go," I said, paying the check. "I can hardly wait to see you in that pink thong," I lied.

Back home, she retreated to the bathroom to try on her presents. I sat on the edge of the bed and, for the first time, fully grasped my dilemma: I'd started out dating a man, now I was dating a woman; I'd started out as a woman, now I was a man. I practiced stretching my face into an expression of happy surprise. I didn't want any revulsion to show when Melanie emerged.

Finally, she stepped out of the bathroom wearing the black bustier and pink thong edged in black ruffles. As Fram had promised, the mesh expanded to accommodate Mel's "basket."

Her bustier was still loose. "Here, let me lace you up. Turn around." I pulled the strings tight, and she gasped in mock protest. "You want to show off that thirty-two-inch waist, don't you?"

As I made the adjustments, I noticed that Melanie had eliminated all body hair in preparation for this night—chest, stomach, legs, even her pubic area. "My God, did you get a bikini wax?"

"Yeah, do you like it? They call it a 'Brazilian.'"

"You really went all out." Inside, I struggled to come up with the right words to describe what stood before me: my boyfriend, luxuriously lingerie-ed, shaved, and waxed. "Melanie has never looked so . . . smooth, so satiny." Meanwhile, under my pantsuit, I sported white cotton panties, a Maidenform bra, and a far more casual approach to body hair. I felt like Melanie had stolen my girl-ness right out from under me.

She made three slow revolutions, modeling her outfit from all angles, while she studied herself in the full-length mirror. "I love what you bought me. But I'm afraid I'm not filling it out in the right places." She fiddled with her bodice.

"Hold on. I've got the perfect solution."

I ran to my office and pulled out a roll of bubble wrap. I hastily cut two twelve-inch circles. Back in the bedroom, I stuffed the wrap in the shelf bra of her bustier, then stepped back to admire my handiwork. "Now you have perfect double Ds!"

She checked her reflection. "Yes, almost an hourglass." Then, with her hand braced on a cocked hip, she asked, "So am I hot or what?"

I pulled her slowly onto my bed. We lay side by side, giggling.

"I've always fantasized about our becoming lesbian lovers," she whispered. "You know, I don't think it's a coincidence that I'm a very feminine man and you're a very masculine woman. I mean, you're not a girly girl. That's why we get along so well."

I pulled away. She reached under the bed and brought out something wrapped in a towel.

"What's that?"

"What do you think?" Melanie held up a long black rubber dildo.

"Good gracious! Where did that come from?"

"I bought it at a naughty shop."

"But it's so big!" I said. "Where's it gonna fit? No orifice in this bed."

"The store clerk said that 'it's for couples who like a challenge.' That's us, right?"

I buried my face in the pillow to stifle my laughter. Then Melanie slid it in my hand. "It's easy. Just imagine you're the guy." I gingerly grabbed the end. "Go ahead," she said.

I wielded the dildo as best I could. As my neighbors can attest, I did an admirable job, at least for a first attempt. Several slammed their windows shut to protest Melanie's screams of passion. As a lover, she was the very opposite of Mel—wild, out of control, impassioned. Then I heard small popping sounds. As she writhed in pleasure, the bubble wrap stuffed in her bodice started to burst.

"Baby, you're just poppin'," I told her as she climaxed.

After Melanie had recovered, she took the dildo from me. "You're next."

"That's okay. I'll pass." She shrugged, drew a finger along my cheek, then fell asleep. I stood examining her. Her mascara had run. The bubble wrap stuck to her carefully shaved calf. And her unlaced bustier revealed a curveless torso, slightly emaciated from miles of daily cycling.

As I watched her sleep, I could feel disquiet rising. Our relationship wasn't about us, it was all about Melanie. Once again, I found myself sidelined. I fled to the guest room.

The next morning, a light kiss on my cheek woke me. I opened one eye. It was Mel, all vestiges of Melanie scrubbed off his face, dressed in khakis, navy polo shirt, and Nikes. "I wish I could stay, but I'm late."

"To pick up your son?"

"Yes, I have to be there by 10. We're going out for our usual waffles."

From the window, I watched Mel tear out of my driveway. He was driving his Saturn station wagon with his seven-year-old's car seat strapped in the back. He presented a perfect picture of the dutiful dad.

I returned to the scene of the crime, climbed into my rumpled bed, and dialed Neville. "You're not gonna believe what I'm looking at," I began.

"What is it this time?" he asked wearily.

"It's about ten inches long, two inches wide, and black."

"Your new yoga prop?"

"Close. It's a prop alright. I learned to use it last night. There's Astro gel everywhere. My sheets are ruined."

"What happened?"

"Well, Melanie wanted to try out the lingerie I bought her. And we had sex for the first time. I won't go into graphic detail. Let's just say, *she* had a good time."

"Not you?"

"I had to play the guy. It was awful." I stared out the window at the cloudless blue sky. Southern California's weather was so perfect, but it felt out of sync with my inner weather.

"So, it's over?"

"I don't know."

"Oh, I think you *do* know."

Chapter 30

MARRIAGE PROPOSAL

The following week, perhaps worried that he'd gone too far on Valentine's Day, Mel invited me on a decidedly different kind of date. "Wanna come watch me fence?"

I sat in the bleachers of a local fencing studio and observed Mel duel with his longtime instructor. I marveled as he held his left hand gracefully to the side for balance, expertly lunging at his opponent with a rhythmic clank of steel.

Then he led me on a forty-mile bike ride along the ocean from Santa Monica to Huntington Beach. He sweated. He strained against the pedals, thighs and calves flexing.

"Please, Mel, I can't keep up. Let's rest."

When we stopped, he pulled a wrench from his bike bag and adjusted the height of my bicycle seat. "That'll give you more leverage," he explained. Later, he paid for lunch.

Back at my condo, he asked, "Do you have any projects that need doing around the house? I can build shelves, haul stuff to Goodwill. Our time together doesn't always have to be an event."

Clearly, he was trying to prove he was a normal, red-blooded American male. And I bought it. Melanie wasn't taking over. She was just an intermittent guest in our budding romance.

Two weeks later, Mel made me dinner at his place. As we dug into our tortellini, he said, "There's this force, this passion about you."

"What can I say? You bring that out in me."

He nodded. "You're intense, yet I feel so calm in your presence. It's such an odd dichotomy." He stopped eating and looked at me. "This is the relationship I've been wanting all my life but up till now I haven't had the skills to create."

"I feel that way, too," I said, trying to convince myself. "You're terrific . . . as both a man *and* a woman."

He held my gaze for a full minute. He studied me in the same way he had on our second date, right before he'd shared about his cross-dressing. Christmas lights still strung across his neighbor's balcony flashed, changing the lighting on his face from dark to light.

"Laurie, we have so much living to do together. Will you be my bride? Will you marry me?"

I was stunned. I had had no idea this question was coming. We'd known each other for only three months. Wasn't such a big decision premature, especially since we had no idea where Melanie would take us?

"Yes, Mel, yes!" I cried, climbing into his lap. As the words sprang from my lips, all I could think of was how I'd finally been accepted into the club everyone in my family had long since joined. By that time, my parents and brother had been married a combined five times.

The next morning, I called my church to nab the earliest available date at the chapel for our wedding. The ceremony was scheduled for September 8, 2001, nine months away.

"That'll be $1,500," the church's wedding planner told me.

Reeling from sticker shock over the high fee, I needed some fresh air. I decided to walk to Michael's, where I hoped to host the post-wedding meal. I hiked thirteen blocks to the old, well-known restaurant on the Third Street Promenade, a few blocks from the Santa Monica pier. The minute I mentioned "wedding dinner," the maître d' sprang into action, calling the special events coordinator on her cell. The woman—tall, slender, with her shiny brunette hair pulled into a French twist—breezed in the door a few minutes later. She produced a three-ring binder of previous weddings, with each photo of a happy couple carefully encased in a clear plastic sleeve. Then, with a quick flick of her wrist, she switched to a second notebook featuring photographers, florists, videographers, jewelers, even a broker in goody bags.

Sensing I was feeling overwhelmed, she said, "If you want to economize, it's only $150 per head for lunch versus $250 for dinner."

Back home, I went to bed, feeling the flu coming on. When I woke up the next morning, I had two messages on my answering machine—one from the church and the other from Michael's. Deposits totaling $3,000 were due. "Could you drop off the check this week?" each asked politely. I went back to bed, my flu now in full bloom.

I slept fitfully. Whenever I roused myself, I felt like a balloon was growing bigger and bigger inside my chest. I looked around my bedroom. In nine months, my cozy sanctuary would no longer be mine; it would be ours. I had to enjoy my waning days of privacy while I still could. Soon I would no longer have solitude when I prayed, meditated, or penned long passages in my journal. Under the date of each diary entry, I began to write the number of days remaining until the wedding. Like a condemned man counting the days to his execution, I wrote, *270, 269, 268, 267 . . .*

I told myself I was just having pre-wedding jitters. It was only natural after living on my own for so long.

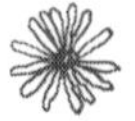

That night, Mel called. "Are you still sick?"

"Yeah, I don't think I can see you this weekend." I spoke in a monotone, trying to sell him on my malaise. The idea of seeing him made me feel even more queasy.

"Why don't we have a slumber party? My son will be with his mother, and the weather report predicts rain, so I most likely won't be cycling. Why don't we climb into our flannel pajamas and just veg for two days?"

My first reaction was, *Whoa, that's a lot of time.* What with his spending time with his son and a rigorous cycling schedule, we had never spent an entire weekend together. But I realized it was time to go into training. Pretty soon we weren't going to spend just a weekend together, we would be spending the rest of our remaining time on earth together. Considering that our grandparents all lived well into their nineties, that meant we would be together every day and night for roughly the next forty to fifty years. I got out my calculator. That meant up to 18,200 days and 18,200 nights. Yikes!

On Friday night, after watching reruns of *The Sopranos*, I retired to my bedroom and Mel to the rollout bed in my den. To carve out some privacy, I had claimed I didn't want to wake him up as I blew my nose or visited the bathroom. I went to bed and stayed there all Friday night and the entire following day—something I had never done in my life. He brought me tea and the newspaper and lay down next to me off and on, pressing his head on my hand like a dog demanding to be petted. He wore brown plaid pajamas Melanie wouldn't have been caught dead in.

"Do you want me to leave?" Mel asked. "It's like you wish I weren't here."

"That's not true at all," I said, actually believing my own words.

When Mel left to rent a video, I stretched out on the bathroom floor and pressed my cheek against the cool tile. I thought the coolness might take away my nausea, but it didn't. I hoisted myself up and leaned over the toilet bowl. I tried to throw up, but just dry-heaved. Flat once again on the ceramic floor, sweating and exhausted, I slowly came to my senses. I didn't really have the flu. I was sick at the idea of marrying Mel. My body was telling me, in the only way it knew how, that the marriage wasn't going to work. I was depressed at the thought of hurting Mel and Melanie, and depressed at the idea of dismantling our relationship. Worst of all, I was depressed at the demise of my lifelong dream of getting married.

Monday morning, after Mel left, I opened my medicine cabinet. He had stashed his toothbrush and toothpaste on the top shelf. I felt like a small animal had built a nest in my ventilation system. It hadn't impeded airflow yet, but, in time, it would. I went back to bed, too sick to go to work.

Then, at 9 a.m., still in my flannel pajamas and slippers, I padded into my office to call the presiding monk at the church. "Mel and I will no longer be having our 11 a.m. wedding on September 8. I'd like to cancel my reservation."

"Thank you for letting us know so far in advance," he said quietly.

Next, I dialed the pretty event planner with the shiny up-do. "I need to cancel dinner for September 8. There's been a change of plans. The wedding's off."

"Oh, no problem," she said warmly. "I totally understand."

On a roll, I made the most difficult call of all. "Mel, we need to talk."

He didn't say anything.

"Let's have dinner tonight at Pradeep's. I'll meet you there at 7 p.m."

"Okay," he said glumly. He sounded like he knew what was coming.

I sat for a long time gazing at my neighbors' backyard below my office window. While I was trashing my marital nest, the couple's spring flowers were blooming. I sat there numb, my ears ringing. Then, slowly, I began to feel this overwhelming relief. I returned to bed vibrating with delicious ecstasy.

Mel and I gave each other a perfunctory hug in the foyer of Pradeep's, then followed the hostess to our seats. Unlike on Valentine's Day, the restaurant was nearly empty. We sat in silence until the waitress came to take our order. Mel tugged on the corners of the pink place mat with his long, graceful fingers. After the waitress left, or rather fled—she seemed to sense something bad was about to happen—I studied Mel a moment. His demeanor was always sober compared with Melanie's. I longed for her to join us, to contribute her ebullience. I wondered if I would ever see her again.

"Mel, I can't marry you," I said.

He was silent for a long time before he finally spoke. "After this weekend, I kind of knew . . ." His voice trailed off.

"I just don't think we work as a couple." What I really wanted to say was as a "threesome," since our association was a ménage à trois composed of Melanie, Mel, and me. But I didn't want to complicate matters. I had a job to do—to definitively end our engagement.

"It's not like it's either of our faults," he said quietly. "I'm actually proud of us, proud of the intimacy we shared."

"I know," I said, starting to cry. "I really tried. We both really tried."

"I'm so glad you spoke up," he said, dabbing his eyes. "You did us a great service, expressing your reservations now and not five years from now. You were really courageous."

I tried to stop crying. "You're so handsome, honorable, sexy, and intelligent, it was hard for me to accept that things didn't feel right."

"Yes, other things, like common interests, might be more important but less apparent," he pointed out.

"I was so blinded by your good qualities, I never considered the fact that we had absolutely nothing in common. Our only real common interest was giving life to Melanie."

"Ah, yes, Melanie . . . She will be forever indebted to you for accepting her with open arms."

Wow, I thought. *This breakup is the most mature one I've ever gone through. I guess I* am *an adult.*

"You're an unusual person, Laurie. You're not normal. But you've spent your whole life trying to fit in, trying to be normal."

This observation stunned me, especially coming from a cross-dresser.

As if reading my mind, he continued. "I'm unusual, too, Laurie. And I've spent my whole life trying to be normal, too. But so often 'being normal' means falling asleep . . . and I wouldn't recommend that for either of us. Maybe that's why Melanie emerged. She personifies all that I've squished down in order to be normal, to be socially acceptable."

"Well, perhaps I have a 'Melanie' stuck inside me, too."

"Yes, I suspect so . . ."

With our time for the evening, and maybe for a lifetime, drawing to a close, Mel flagged the waitress. "Check, please."

Chapter 31

METTLE

After regaling my former coworkers at the convent with how I was about to marry this tall, handsome man in the church's chapel, I was too embarrassed to tell them I had broken our engagement. But highly perceptive Selma knew something was up.

Over a lunch of pad Thai, she observed, "You seemed more and more pinched these past few weeks, Laurie. Now you seem lighter, more relaxed, more open. Did you come to some decision?"

Obviously, I couldn't hide my news. "Yeah, I called off the wedding. Mel and I are over."

"Good!" Bettina called from the other end of the table. "Your complexion was starting to look really bad. Your energy wasn't flowing. We want the juicy Laurie back!"

I was astounded that my inner turmoil was so apparent to others. But once I'd called off the wedding, even strangers seemed to notice. When I picked up a pizza at my favorite Italian restaurant, the cook yelled from the back of the kitchen, "Hey, love ya!" The clerk at Barnes & Noble smiled at me and asked how my day was going. Even neighbors who rarely acknowledged me started wishing me a good morning.

But in spite of encouraging words from friends and coworkers, I still felt enormous doubt about my decision. Maybe I'd gotten cold feet. Maybe I was really afraid of the deep intimacy marriage represented to me.

Several months had passed after our breakup at Pradeep's, and Mel and I hadn't spoken once. I decided to arrange a meeting. Although I felt uncomfortable at the thought of seeing him again, of opening the wound, I needed to know if I had made the right decision. We agreed to meet for an early Friday dinner at the Fig Tree, an outdoor café on the Venice boardwalk.

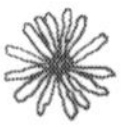

I got there early and grabbed a table near the ocean. The roar of the crashing waves, I hoped, would smooth the jagged edges of our conversation. Mel sauntered down the boardwalk in his graceful, loose-limbed way, wearing khaki clam diggers, orange tennis shoes, and mirrored shades. Noting the sapphire studs sparkling in each ear, I wondered if Melanie had come instead. But when he got closer, I was disappointed to discover that he'd come as Mel.

The waitress gave us menus. We didn't look at them. The sun was low on the horizon, bathing the beach in bright orange light. What looked like a homeless man sat on the boardwalk wall, strumming amazingly well on a guitar. The scene felt uncomfortably romantic.

I broke the silence first. "How have you been? How has Melanie been?"

He took off his sunglasses, revealing red-rimmed eyes as if he'd been crying. "I didn't sign any new clients on my last business trip.

I'm tired of playing the 'walking wallet': child support, alimony, payroll for a staff of five, not to mention my office and apartment rents. And, unless you're around, Melanie stays in her box."

I felt sympathy, but also unease. He appeared to be the very man he'd presented at the beginning of our relationship—a three-antidepressant-a-day guy.

I stared at the menu and then my chopped salad throughout the meal. We made small talk, avoiding the elephant in the room—our broken engagement. Hoping for some semblance of connection, I suggested window shopping on Main Street after dinner. He half-heartedly agreed.

We stopped at the boutique where we'd once bought a blouse for Melanie. "Remember?" I said, pointing to a mannequin wearing a top similar to his silk shell.

He nodded, barely looking at the display.

After a few more futile attempts at conversation, we walked in stony silence. We finally arrived back at the Fig Tree's parking lot. At my car, he turned away without a hug, a goodbye, or even his trademark handshake. Then he disappeared into the night.

I drove home cringing at how the evening had unraveled.

Five days later, a letter arrived, the envelope addressed in Mel's small, cramped handwriting. With trepidation, I tore it open.

Mel thanked me for bringing Melanie into the world: "I shall be forever grateful to you." Then came the slap: "I hope one day you are ready for the marriage contract."

He made no mention of the complete lack of commonalities that we'd discussed at Pradeep's. Instead, he made it sound like, currently, I didn't have the mettle for the demands of marital commitment. That was the real reason I had broken off our engagement. I was crushed. Was he right?

Near tears, I called Neville to ask what I should do about Mel's letter.

"He makes marriage sound like a business arrangement," Neville observed. "You know, pony up your investment and sign on the dotted line."

"Well, marriage *is* an arrangement," I pointed out, "a contract of sorts."

"You mean, till death do us part?"

"Yeah, *that* vow, but also the fine print that no one bothers to read."

"What's the fine print in the marriage contract Mel proposed?"

"Oh, my beloved bride, stay just as cheerful as you are. That dulls my psychic pain." I was surprised at my rancor. "Have lots of sex with me, too. Both your cheer and sex will serve as antidepressants to add to my current three a day. Let me live relatively rent-free in the condo that you own. What with alimony, child support, student loans, and staff payroll, I don't have much to contribute. And one last thing: Drop all hope of my joining you at church. I don't want you to even talk about all that nonsense."

"That's harsh."

"Well, that's why the fine print is left unspoken."

"But what does Mel give you as part of the deal?"

"The status of marriage to a tall, well-dressed, employed man. Hell, by societal standards isn't that enough for a woman pushing fifty?"

"And love? Or dare I ask?"

"Mel told me he never loved his first wife. I suspect he didn't love me so much as need me for the aforementioned reasons."

"Oh boy," Neville said, letting out a long exhalation.

"Thanks for listening, Neville. Now I know I made the right decision to call off the engagement."

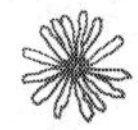

The next day, I told Bettina about Mel's letter. I had regaled her with our ongoing saga in weekly phone calls.

"I don't think the marriage Mel proposed was right for you," she observed. "He needs to deepen his relationship with Melanie. And maybe you need to deepen the relationship with your own self, with your own version of Melanie. Otherwise, you'll always play the sidekick, never the main attraction."

Bettina was right. "Sidekick" was the appropriate label for me. Speed cycling, cross-dressing as Melanie, clinging to his persistent sadness and solid antidepressant regime had all served as Mel's main attractions.

In the subsequent months, I soothed my disappointment with multiple classes at Yoga Works. Then one day, as I headed out the door, my yoga mat rolled under my arm, a man zoomed by on a bike. It took me a second to recognize him. It was Mel, riding his favorite fifteen-speed orange bike and wearing matching orange goggles.

It was the last time I would ever see him . . . or Melanie. I should have felt sad; instead, I felt immense relief. By avoiding my vow to Mel, I had renewed the vow to myself.

Chapter 32

BLUNT FORCE TRAUMA

"Time out," Neville recommended. I agreed wholeheartedly. My relationships seemed only to be getting worse with time. But alone one night after work, my curiosity got the better of me. I broke my "time out" mandate and looked up Jonathan. No, I didn't call or email him. I wasn't that stupid. Instead, I looked him up on my favorite people-finder website. Was he still living in that house with the dirt front yard? Had his "dear princess" moved in?

Considering his behavior following our second date, I doubted he would ever find "the one." A week after our aborted weekend, Jonathan had left a phone message, screaming, "You two-faced, lying scum!!" My heart started pounding. I wondered if I should delete the message or save it as evidence to support a restraining order.

Eight days later, on February 14, a large box arrived. I wondered if I should fetch a box cutter or call the bomb squad. I decided to take a chance and ripped it open. Inside was a Valentine's Day gift—a giant stuffed teddy bear with a pink Post-it note stuck to its forehead. The note read: "I'm feeling horrible all squished in this box unable to give my love."

I immediately drove to Goodwill to drop off the bear. Even though I'd never divulged my address, his package proved that he knew where I lived, right down to my nine-digit zip code. From then on, I feared opening my front door, not to mention my mailbox.

A few months later, Jonathan left another message: "I miss you, girl. I really had a good time with you. But there's clearly no desire on your part. So I've decided to call and say goodbye. Goodbye, Laurie."

Good riddance!

I typed Jonathan's name, age, and city in the query box of the people-finder site. To my horror, written in tiny red letters next to his name were the words "Died, February 10, 2000." I felt like a detective who had just unearthed the pivotal clue in a cold case. But I also had to remind myself that the internet was not always reliable. For all I knew, Jonathan was alive and kicking. To learn if he really was dead, I signed up for trial accounts with other people-finder sites. The services did not confirm his death, but they did provide more information, like his mother's maiden name and birthplace. I now had enough data to fill out a death certificate request.

Within twenty-four hours of placing my order with San Diego Vital Records, strange things began to happen. When I turned on my bedside lamp, the light bulb burst. The clicker that had consistently locked my car for a decade suddenly failed. And a bottle of hair oil slipped from my hand, shattered on the bathroom floor, and stained my new slippers.

Bad luck? Or was the Senator of the Spiritual Realm angry at my meddling and toying with me from the other side?

The death certificate arrived in the mail ten days later. Standing at my kitchen counter, I slowly opened the envelope. Under "Cause of Death," the coroner had typed: "Blunt force trauma to head and trunk."

"My God! Jonathan was murdered!" I called out to the empty room.

I continued reading. For "Manner of Death," an "X" had been typed in the box for "Suicide." Under "Describe events which resulted in injury" was "Decedent drove his vehicle off a 400 ft. cliff, died of injuries sustained in accident." It even gave the exact GPS coordinates of the crash.

On Google Earth, I found the location of the accident. It was at the lip of the Mojave, where the green of the Cleveland National Forest quickly turns to the tan of the desert. I imagined Jonathan had wound through the lush countryside until he hit what looked like the surface of the moon. After a few miles, he noted that the cliffs rose high enough to drive off without surviving. That's when he'd swerved the wheel of his car, most likely the Camry he'd driven me in to and from the Del Mar train station.

Jonathan had nearly died in a car crash seven years before we met. That's how he'd explained his misshapen little finger and the pins in his back. Perhaps that crash had not been an accident, but actually a failed suicide attempt.

I recalled a documentary I'd once watched about near-death experiences. Those who'd died and come back to life often shared Jonathan's life ambition. Having enjoyed complete and unconditional love in death, they returned to life determined to create more light and love—just as he hoped to in his assigned role as Senator of the Spiritual Realm and united with his "dear princess."

I studied the date of death: "FND 02/10/2000." His body had been found four days before Valentine's Day. I suspected his search for a princess had proven fruitless, and facing one more February 14 alone too much to bear.

As the horror of the news sank in, I realized Jonathan and I were a lot alike. We shared a feverish quest to mate—one that led to dire circumstances. For the past two decades, my romantic pursuits had siphoned off untold amounts of my time, energy, mindshare, and equanimity. Even worse, my failure to find the right partner had eroded my self-worth. Maybe I hadn't found him for a good reason: I wasn't fun enough, sexy enough, or accommodating enough. If I were, I would have found him by now. Equally damaging, I'd lived much of my life in a waiting room, believing all activities, whether leisure, professional, or avocational, would truly come alive in joy and meaning only once I'd gotten married. I hadn't driven off a cliff, but my pursuit of a "dear prince" had trashed my life in other ways. I vowed, *no more.*

Chapter 33

MELTDOWN

The astrologer at the Temple of the Reclining Buddha had been sorely mistaken about my matrimonial prospects. After my experiences with Jonathan and Mel, I hunkered down at home, someplace quiet and safe where I could regroup.

As I prepared Friday supper, I noticed tiny trails of steam pouring from the wall sockets in my kitchen. My neighbor is simply running her dishwasher, I reasoned. But when the plumes thickened, I realized the vapor wasn't steam; it was smoke.

"Get out! Get out now!" a woman screamed as she pounded on my door.

I flung the door open. There was Sherry, the high school principal who lived next door with her adopted daughter.

"My condo's on fire!" she cried, yanking my hand.

We ran down the complex's bumpy side path, our hands outstretched for balance. As we passed Units #3, #2, and #1, we yelled, "Get out! Get out!"

Sirens grew louder as two fire engines careened down Sycamore. At the street curb, Sherry and I waved our arms wildly over our heads to flag down the fire trucks.

Out of breath, Sherry explained to the fire captain: "My french fries caught on fire. I tried to put it out with my fire extinguisher, but the flames grew out of control."

Six firemen raced past us with hoses. A crowd gathered on the street to watch the flames shoot from the complex roof—the roof that the HOA had just replaced at great expense. I couldn't fathom how a pan of french fries could create a two-story-high fire.

In an hour, the fire had been extinguished. I wanted to return to my unit, but the fire chief stopped me. "Your home is filled with off-gases." He handed me a gas mask and asked a crewman to escort me to collect a few belongings.

I picked through my closet in the dark. Everything was slightly damp from the fire hoses. I fished out a small avocado Samsonite suitcase in the corner. I packed plaid flannel pajamas, my diary, and a toothbrush. The fireman carried my suitcase as he led me out of my unit.

I walked two blocks up the main drag of Wilshire, the wheels of my suitcase clicking on the sidewalk.

The desk clerk at the Comfort Inn said, "You smell like smoke."

"Yeah, my place just burned down," I replied, exaggerating a little.

"I'm so sorry," she said. "I'll upgrade you. No charge. It has a kitchenette you might need."

I hung up my smoky overcoat in the closet and sat on the edge of the king-size bed. I called State Farm. "I'm so sorry," the agent for the complex said. Later, the agent for my own unit said, "I'm so sorry." Neville, my brother, and my mother also said, "I'm so sorry."

The mandatory calls completed, I climbed into my pajamas and sat cross-legged on the massive bed, leaning against the velvet headboard. My ears still rang with the sirens, my neighbor's screams, and the pounding water from the hoses. Everyone was sorry. As the din in my ears subsided, I realized *I* wasn't sorry. I wasn't sorry at all.

The next day, I ventured back to my home to assess the damage. The disaster crew, in bright yellow vests, were already hard at work. They had piled my kitchen cabinets—now burned rubble—in the tiny interior patio. They'd ripped out my wall-to-wall beige carpet, exposing the bare cement subfloor in the living and dining rooms. They'd poured my possessions—shampoo, shoes, yoga mat—indiscriminately in large black plastic bags. Giant air purification fans roared in every room.

I poked my head in my closet to collect a change of clothes.

"Oh, we've sent your wardrobe to the ozone chamber," a worker told me. "You know, to de-smoke." My condo had become part of the catastrophe industrial complex.

I peeked into my office, afraid of the destruction I might find. My three hundred diaries still lined the floor-to-ceiling shelves; my most cherished possessions had been spared. I asked the disaster crew to deliver the volumes to my car trunk. I wanted to read them before another catastrophe took them out. I suspected they had been spared for a good reason.

I called State Farm to ask what happened next.

"Well, first off, in handling this claim, you can't serve in this case as both HOA president and homeowner. That's a conflict of interest."

I hung up the phone and drafted my resignation. Finally, I'd found the perfect escape from my tenure as HOA president.

As I left the war zone and returned to the Comfort Inn, a surprising elation came over me. Why, I wasn't sure.

That night, I sat at the tiny desk in the corner of my motel room, my leather-bound diary splayed open in front of me. I wrote the date at the top of the page—*April 7, 2001*. Sometimes, so much happened in one day, I didn't know how to start my daily entry. To buy more time, I added *Comfort Inn, Room 206, 9:15 p.m.* under the date. I waited for the words to come.

> *God lit a match. I totaled my car. I broke up with my fiancé. And now my home burned down. I suspect all this destruction is the Divine saying, "Move on, girl. Nothing is working out—not how you drive, not who you date, and not where you live. The whole enchilada is poisoned. Let me help you along by destroying every last shred of your life."*

I shut the diary, tucked into bed, and slept like a baby.

Chapter 34

BACHELOR PAD

I liked Room 206, with its corner desk, kitchenette stocked with complimentary cocoa, and view of a small, turquoise pool. The space didn't swallow me the way my condo had. The motel room was designed for one guest, two at most. I had no qualms about sticking with these modest digs while I rebuilt my condo.

That is, until my brother Peter called with an invitation. "Come live with me. The dogs would love it."

Many viewed my brother, Peter, a handsome million-dollar-a-year cinematographer, as a typical Hollywood bachelor. After a short marriage in his twenties, he'd played the field for sixteen years. Horseback riding with Bo Derek on his forty-fourth birthday. Vacationing in Venice with a Dallas Cowboys cheerleader. And bedding a Calvin Klein underwear model after a film shoot in the Moroccan desert.

I didn't fit into his ranch house in the Valley, with a Blackberry constantly buzzing, a sunken living room swimming with the ghosts of his seductions, and a backyard pool where I'd once caught his women friends sunbathing topless.

"Thanks for the offer," I said. "Let me sleep on it."

The next morning, as I stretched out on my California king, I considered Peter's suggestion. The mention of his dogs had piqued my interest. Right now, I could be snuggling in bed with them.

I dialed Peter. "Is the offer still good?"

"Definitely! I'll leave the key under the ficus. Come any time today."

Later that afternoon, my avocado suitcase in tow, I appeared at Peter's door. His dogs wagged their tails so hard, their whole bodies wiggled. Husky Shane howled with pleasure. Retriever Rex welcomed me by gently holding my forearm in his mouth.

Peter was out for the evening, so I scrounged leftover pasta from his fridge, then settled into his guest bedroom. I sat cross-legged, leaning against the headboard to meditate. Rex slept with his chin resting on my knee. Shane curled up at the end of the bed, his snout pointing straight down into a pile of clothes.

Fifteen minutes later, the bed began to vibrate. *Maybe it's an earthquake or a truck driving by,* I thought. I opened my eyes. Shane's paws twitched as he ran in his dreams. Rex's head was still on my knee. Hanging with these dogs felt so consoling. I needed their uncomplicated affection—which was so hard for me to find with my own species.

Even though I hadn't lived with Peter for almost two decades, we quickly fell into a comfortable routine. At our first breakfast together—eggs and bacon for Peter and shredded wheat cereal for me—our phones rang simultaneously. We laughed at our chorus of pings.

"This is Collister and Collister Marketing," I said to a pretend customer before answering.

"I'm sure you need some toner," Peter said into his Blackberry.

Later, Peter called from the supermarket. "Hey, Laur, should I buy the milk chocolate or dark chocolate schoolboy cookies?" He was referring to the iced shortbread treats our mother used to have waiting for us after school.

In the late afternoons, Peter often invited me to join him and one or more of "Los Tres Pedros"—his three best friends were named Peter, too—as we exercised the dogs on a hike through Runyon Canyon. One time, I hid a bottle of Pellegrino and plastic champagne glasses in my backpack. A stray hiker, the three Pedros, my brother and I toasted his forty-sixth birthday on a cliff overlooking the city.

"Peter said he likes having you live at his house," Mom told me. I was so happy to hear he didn't view me as a burden.

As the weeks at Peter's unfolded, I could feel my body change. My skin looked less blotchy. The persistent squeeze in my gut loosened. I realized I was responding to the experience of living, for the first time in thirty-five years, in a real home, where a neighbor drops by to borrow an egg, where a dog pokes his nose in my ribs for a pat, where there are always sounds—coffee beans grinding, half of a phone conversation, dogs barking. I felt like I had five hundred more watts of energy at my disposal. I hadn't realized just how much energy I had diverted to assuaging my loneliness, not to mention settling for romantic mismatches.

Since my clothes were still in an ozone chamber at some undisclosed location in Burbank, I'd begun to run out of things to wear. When State Farm sent a reimbursement check for $500, I headed to Fashion Square, returning with a bag of pajamas, T-shirts, a sweater, joggers, flip-flops, even a toy for the dogs—a glow-in-the-dark rubber ball.

As I laid my purchases on the bed, Peter surveyed my haul. "Wow, Laur, everything's pink!" I hadn't noticed that, but yes, the cardigan from J. Crew was shell pink; the flip-flops, shocking pink; and the Buddy Glow Ball, bubblegum pink. I tried to understand my color choice. Then it dawned on me: pink, the color of cotton candy and valentines, perfectly captured how I was feeling.

At a psychic fair sponsored by my alma mater, the psychic institute in Santa Monica, my clairvoyant described my current life as filled with "yumminess." She explained that the feeling represented a carryover from a previous life when I was a seventeen-year-old in love. While I couldn't vouch for my previous incarnation, I concurred with her description of my current state. In a finger snap, my whole life had changed for the better . . . and through no effort of my own other than my unconscious desire to leave my condo and my former life.

But all was not cotton candy and valentines. I had also stepped into what felt like a *Seinfeld* episode. Juggling multiple girlfriends, Peter accidentally left a message intended for Molly on Rose's cell. In a panic, Peter did what George Costanza would have done—hack into Rose's phone to delete the message.

A few days later, Molly, a thirty-nine-year-old newscaster, arrived for a date and announced, "We can do this either the natural way or this way." She whipped a turkey baster out of her Louis Vuitton. She wanted a baby before it was too late.

In the meantime, Rose, a pretty, twenty-four-year-old barista, was about to be evicted from her studio apartment. Would Peter help her make this month's rent? Just this once?

I felt very Jane Austen—the spinster sister quietly sewing in her attic bedroom. I overheard conversations, yet I said not a word. It was not my place. Besides, I was too busy luxuriating in the exotic, consoling experience of living in a home.

A few weeks later, Peter arrived at the house, grasping his stomach and hyperventilating. His fingertips tingled. His face turned white. He felt nauseated. Was it food poisoning? The flu? A heart attack? We didn't know. I dialed 911.

Within minutes, three strapping paramedics tore through the front door, while the dogs barked frantically in my bedroom, where I'd shut them away, safe from the fray. The medics pasted electrodes to Peter's chest. They took his blood pressure and temperature. All his vitals proved normal. "Mr. Collister is having a panic attack," one said flatly.

Unconvinced, I ordered Peter's transport to the nearest hospital. Gunning my car to keep up with the ambulance, I made it to the exam room to talk with the cardiologist on call. He concurred with the paramedics' assessment. "Do you know how many people in Hollywood have panic attacks every day?" He slammed Peter's chart shut. "A lot!"

I could see that all was not as it seemed in Peter's sun-dappled bachelor pad. I suggested he lay low over the weekend, perhaps forgoing female companionship. He agreed, inviting his best friend from grade school, Ethan, and Ethan's nine-month-old son, Harry, to catch a game on TV. I watched Peter hold Harry, carefully cupping a napkin under his dripping ice cream sucker. Peter's arms, nicked and tanned from long days on movie sets, contrasted with the little boy's creamy, translucent skin. As he carefully held the child, I could see someone who would make a good father. I had never bought his eternal Hollywood bachelor guise. At heart, Peter was a family man. He wanted what Ethan enjoyed—a loving marriage and children.

Another check from State Farm arrived. It was for $158,000, the total designated to rebuild my condo. I had to lie down. The check spelled the end of my newfound happier life. Six months had passed since the January fire and I had not hired a single contractor to lay tile or install cabinets. I had no interest in returning to my former life. I wanted more, a whole lot more.

Chapter 35

FIFTY SHADES OF BEIGE

I wanted to live with Peter forever. I couldn't imagine sleeping without Rex and Shane stretched out next to me. Or writing in my diary without the hubbub of a household outside my door. Or forgoing afternoon hikes in Runyon Canyon.

A friend I hadn't seen in awhile remarked, "You look better than I've ever seen you. Have you had some work done?"

"It's what's known as happiness," I explained. "That's the work I've had done."

I hadn't realized how much pain I'd been in living alone until it suddenly ended upon my move to Peter's. Was I destined to return to that same pain when I moved back into my condo?

Of course, I couldn't stay at Peter's forever. The rent State Farm paid to Peter—$1,500 a month—was set to end soon. And I felt stupid paying a sizable mortgage on a burned-out shell of a condo. But what really got me were my mother's words, straight out of a Jane Austen novel: "One mustn't take advantage of a brother's kindness."

I tried to console myself, remembering what Peter had once shared: "My house has always been my sanctuary, my place to find peace. And your living here has not disturbed that peace." Maybe it would be okay if I stayed just a little while longer.

Periodically I'd visit my condo. The firemen had left sooty footprints on the beige carpet. The air smelled of smoke and mildew. The clean-up crew had dumped my possessions willy-nilly in large cardboard boxes—cosmetics on top of books, on top of altar ornaments, on top of paper clips. Unpacking would take days, if not weeks, of laborious organization. I imagined the army of carpet installers, painters, and tile layers I'd have to hire to make my condo whole. *Oh Lordy,* I'd think, as I locked the door and drove off. *I'll tackle it next week.* Then, in subsequent visits, I'd cycle through the identical drill and inertia.

Finally, I acknowledged I needed to call in reinforcements. Zelda would know what to do. In an email, I explained the problem: my reluctance to devote hundreds of hours to refurbishing a condo I never wanted to see again.

"Simple," Zelda said. "We'll fix it up and sell it for three times what you paid for it!"

With a pocket notebook in hand, I trailed Zelda around my condo, recording changes I needed to make to earn "top dollar"—hardwood floors instead of carpet, granite instead of tile counters, and a coat of "Navajo White" paint on all walls. Her handpicked contractors called the next day.

I visited stone yards to select a slab of granite—an easy choice of black with gold speckles for the kitchen counters. But choosing tile for the kitchen and bathroom floors proved more problematic. There were fifty shades of beige, not to mention a variety of numbers assigned to indicate skid-proof quotients. When I laid out samples on the kitchen table later that night to get Peter's opinion, he ran out of the room crying, "Oh God, Laur, you decide."

Installation demanded even more time. The slab of perfect black granite broke, not once, but twice. The tilers didn't lay the squares diagonally as directed. Back I flew to the northern reaches of the San Fernando Valley to repurchase more material.

I took Shane and Rex along to inspect the jobs. I needed their moral support. Some contractors were nonverbal, barely able to engage in any discourse about their assignment. Others came on to me: "You know, ma'am, I have to tell you, I wish I could be your dog."

Within two months, Zelda deemed my condo salable. During the first open house, on a Sunday afternoon, I parked in front of my complex and watched prospective buyers, neighbors, and lookie-loos parade in and out of my unit, like scavengers inspecting a kill. In spite of the $150,000 renovation, the condo's slip still showed: the mildew-stained grout in the basement, the 1970s linoleum in the guest bathroom, and a fireplace screen that had seen better days.

But that apparently mattered little. Bids poured in, tens of thousands of dollars over the asking price. One prospective buyer sent drawings of my condo crayoned by his three children, along with letters written in wobbly block letters, explaining how much they wanted to live there. A former Miss California, a Pfizer executive, and a child psychiatrist also jockeyed to submit the winning bid.

Eventually I accepted the Pfizer exec's bid, at a selling price nearly four times what I'd initially paid for the condo. Amazingly, it had appreciated $1,250 each and every week for years. I felt like my abusive husband had suddenly died and left me a ton of money. The American dream of home ownership had turned out to be as flawed as my other dream of finding true happiness with a man.

Chapter 36

ZELDA

In short order, escrow closed and I drove home with an $899,000 check burning a hole in my purse. Zelda immediately scrolled through multiple real estate listings to find a way to spend said check. I showed her the kind of house I was looking for—a 1920s Spanish bungalow two doors down from my brother. Every afternoon walking Rex and Shane, I stopped and admired its red-tiled roof, stained glass windows, and a pink crape myrtle tree in the front yard. I could live there, I said over and over, as the dogs yanked on their leashes to continue their walk.

Within a day, Zelda called. "I've arranged for you to buy that very house!" The owners, a young couple, had just filed for divorce. *A coincidence*, I wondered, *or had some divine powers been at work?*

The owners gave me twenty-four hours to decide before they put their house on the market. I'd normally take a week debating whether to buy a $98 dress and here I had one day to decide whether to spend $945,000.

The next morning, I gingerly knocked on the door. The seller's real estate agent said "hello" in a lilting British accent. A light rain pattered on the living room windows, making the space feel warm and protective. One bedroom overlooked a lemon tree, heavy with plump, rain-splattered fruit. Best of all, the house was only a fifteen-second walk away to see Peter, Rex, and Shane.

"I'll take it," I said.

The next day, disoriented by my massive snap decision, I forgot to put quarters in the parking meter, or turn off the car's interior light, or call a friend at our agreed-upon time.

I clung to my remaining thirty days at Peter's house before escrow closed. I tried not to dwell on the cruel reality that my cozy existence as I knew it would end soon.

But end it did. I cried, and I rarely cried, as I moved boxes from Peter's house to my new home. The dogs joined me, racing from room to room, sniffing every square inch. But then they whimpered at the front door. They didn't want to spend too much time in this strange space. They wanted to return to their own home.

The first night, I slept in the room where the couple's young sons had slept in twin beds. I preferred their smaller space. It didn't overwhelm me like the master bedroom with its cathedral ceilings. The boys had left their ceiling fixture—a pale blue glass sphere, painted with clouds—and dresser pulls in the shape of airplanes, baseballs, and pinwheels. They'd left their energy, too. I piggybacked on their warmth and ebullience, just as I'd absorbed the same feelings in Peter's home. I hoped one day I could imprint the space with my own good vibrations.

Chapter 37

NOW WHAT

It was sad that I was no longer living with Peter, but I had to admit, compared with a few years earlier, my home life had improved immensely. I'd traded an acrimonious condo for a far more serene Spanish bungalow that I could manage without the onus of group consensus. Even better, I'd traded neighbors who wanted me to manage the damn HOA, and little else, for a brother two doors down who invited me over for a drink and two dogs happy to cuddle and join me for a walk.

Now I needed to reconfigure my profession, too. Freelance writing had become just as alienating as my dating curriculum. The jobs were nothing short of soul-sucking. Take my HMO client. At first, I wrote diabetes and heart disease brochures. Not particularly interesting, but I could handle those assignments. Then, my duties took a sharp left turn—penning three thousand "Dear John" letters to the HMO's patients. As the economy took a turn for the worse, many Angelenos lost their jobs and, in turn, their health insurance. I had to write something to the effect of "Sorry, dude, you, your three children and mother-in-law have all lost your health insurance. Call us when you're solvent again."

"Maintain our brand voice and style," my boss urged. "Keep the tone warm and friendly. Most of all, present an optimistic future."

And I won't even go into my VoIP client in Czechoslovakia who hired me to place stories in European media about the client's cost-saving telephone technology. Calling editors in Berlin at 3 a.m. on a scratchy VoIP phone line . . . well, it made the "Dear John" assignment seem like a good gig.

I found solace in my garage. In contrast to my writing assignments, the task of unpacking the mountain of boxes remaining from my move was concrete and clear. Even better, I found tidbits of wisdom buried in the jumble.

A book called *Creating Sacred Space with Feng Shui* pointed out: "Think what happens when a pool of water stagnates. Very soon it becomes murky and starts to smell." Exactly! I would not allow a large swath of my life to stay smelly and murky! Cleaning the garage was a start.

A manila folder held mission statements I'd drafted as an Artist's Way workshop in-class assignment. Over the years, I had refined my statement into one short phase: "Heal with words."

A box of school documents proved equally illuminating. My second-grade teacher at Gates Mills Elementary—a red brick schoolhouse on top of a hill with a buckeye tree in front –wrote this in my end-of-the-year report card: "Laurie is a good girl, but she is not with us. Frequently, we catch her staring off into space. Where she is, we do not know."

My father called it my "brown study" and, later, a therapist referred to it as "your occasional disassociation." But maybe a college psychology professor explained it best. In my semester evaluation, he wrote, "Ms. Collister doesn't understand how unique she is and then she wonders why she doesn't fit in. Instead of struggling to be normal, which she will never achieve, she needs to capitalize on her differentness and, I might add, on her goodness."

My boxes of diaries stacked high in the corner of the garage reflected the truth of that professor's assessment. Every week, I retrieved seven journals from the garage, maintaining my quota of reading one volume per day. In the thousands of entries, I observed myself work hard to be normal—to marry, to bear children, to form a family. As society directed, I looked to men to complete me. Yet the very opposite occurred—they depleted me.

Now what? What the hell did the professor mean when he advised that I "capitalize on my differentness"?

As I struggled to answer that question, I came upon my most enlightening find of the day—my birth certificate. The six-by-eight-inch piece of parchment featured a pen-and-ink drawing of the small army hospital in Lawton, Oklahoma, where I was born. A gleaming gold seal, the foil surprisingly intact after almost fifty years, gave it gravitas. At the bottom, the attending physician had written in a careful blue script: "Born alive." Her description of me—a ten-minute-old, squirming pink creature—permeated me for days.

Chapter 38

WIVES OF COLFAX MEADOWS

Now that I was an official homeowner, I set about bonding with my new neighborhood. Online, I researched its history. In 1924, developers had purchased a one-mile-square parcel of land in the San Fernando Valley that was covered with sycamores, palms, and orange trees. Over the next decade, they'd built sprawling ranch-style homes and tiny Spanish bungalows like mine, billing the development "Colfax Meadows."

Soon a film studio, which eventually became CBS, built its facility next door. In turn, the neighborhood attracted luminaries like Clark Gable and, later, Leonardo DiCaprio and Prince. When fan mail appeared in my mailbox, I learned another star had moved in, too. The actress who played the feisty, spoiled heiress on a 1980s soap opera had once lived in my house.

My cul-de-sac, which ended at the banks of the LA River, teemed with a stream of joggers, roller bladers, baby strollers, and dogs on their daily constitutional. A handsome teenage boy across the street shot hoops in his driveway every afternoon. Children splashed in the backyard pool next door.

Unlike in Santa Monica, where my hellos often met with blank stares, in Colfax Meadows every passerby spoke to me. Sometimes I had to fight back tears at the unexpected display of friendliness. Of course, walking Rex and Shane helped. "Your dogs are so cute!" children called out. "Can we pet them?" Their parents stopped to chat while their children knelt to stroke the dogs.

My former housemates—Peter and the dogs—immediately made me feel like "su casa es mi casa." Peter would pad over in his bare feet and boxers to borrow bread to make French toast. As I journaled in the backyard, Rex retrieved kindling from behind the garage to gnaw on. Shane set about to dig a hole. "Shane, what are you doing?" I scolded. He stopped and looked at me. "Ah, go ahead," I relented. "Make yourself at home." He continued to dig and then stretched out for a nap in the cool, damp earth.

Had I moved onto a stage set? With every prop, every backdrop, every actor perfectly choreographed to portray the ultimate white picket fence community that I'd always dreamed of joining? After all, Colfax Meadows literally *was* a stage set. Just two blocks away, Paramount Pictures had shot *The Brady Bunch*, the iconic 1970s TV show about a blended family of six children. Tourists often photographed the split-level, ranch-style home used for the show's exterior scenes.

Colfax Meadows also hosted shows of a more salacious nature. My neighbor Robert Blake, who played the street-smart cop in another iconic 1970s series, *Baretta,* was accused of murdering his wife, Bonnie Lee, outside an Italian restaurant less than a mile from my house. Word had it, he'd hired a hit man. *The Brady Bunch* had to step aside for an episode of *Desperate Housewives.* On a walk after the mysterious shooting, the dogs and I stopped at the dumpster where the murder weapon had been tossed. I peered inside. Maybe the cops had missed some other key evidence.

On my daily walks with the dogs, I'd stumble on a film crew shooting a commercial, TV show, or film. The bustling mini-city of actors and grips, gaffers and DPs, caterers, and security guards dominated an entire block with costume, equipment, and catering trucks. Once, a caterer offered the dogs a tray of leftover fish tacos. Shane sniffed the pan, wild-eyed at his good fortune. "Thanks for the offer," I said, tugging on his leash. "I think we'll pass."

One location manager knocked on my door and offered me $1,000 to rent my twelve-foot driveway for the day. "We need it to shoot stills," he explained. When I stared at him, dumbfounded at his proposition, he assumed I was playing hardball. "How 'bout $1,500?" he countered. "Would that be okay?" "It's a deal," I said, happy at the sudden contribution to my mortgage payments.

I studied the Wives of Colfax Meadows, hoping to learn the passcode to their comfortable domesticity. Jennica, who lived in a McMansion next door, represented what many men might consider ideal: a petite, blonde USC grad in her early thirties. A freelance interior designer, Jennica was forever redesigning her home—changing the knickknacks, carpeting, paint, and window treatments. After she gave birth to her second child, she planted a six-foot stork in her front lawn, "It's a Boy!" painted in blue script across the bundle hanging from the bird's beak.

Jennica retrieved her newspaper at 6 a.m., her hair, even at that early hour, a freshly blown-out, bouncy bob. I commissioned Peter to learn the secret of her hairstyle; he was good at things like that. Soon I was sitting in the chair of Jennica's hairdresser, Tawny, at a mini-mall down the street. While Tawny did not transform my hair into Jennica's Mount Everest of styles, my cut and color, highlights and shine definitely improved.

Across the street, May, the mother of a ten- and thirteen-year-old, was forever leaping into her SUV and tearing out the drive. Even though her driveway was on a short, sharp incline, she expertly backed the car into the drive when she returned home. Poised for the most expeditious of exits, nose pointed toward the street, the vehicle represented, in my mind, May's just-do-it-now-ness. By contrast, I'd spend five minutes before taking off in my Corolla, making sure I had my wallet, grocery list, checkbook, cell phone, glasses, notepad, pen, and reading material, then running a grounding cord from the bottom of my car to the center of the earth. "That'll help you steer clear of accidents," my teacher in psychic college had pointed out.

To hell with all that. I set about to duplicate May's lightning-fast exit, hoping, in the process, that some of her pragmatism would rub off on me. I slowly backed my car into the driveway so its front pointed toward the street just like May's Range Rover. As I climbed in the car the next morning, headed to the post office, I turned on the ignition and accelerated after barely shutting the door. Forgetting the narrowness of my stone gate, built in the 1920s, I ripped off my sideview mirror. My attempt to copy May had ended, literally, out of the starting gate.

As the Wives of Colfax Meadows walked their dogs or pushed their grandchildren in strollers, they'd stop to chat. Turns out, they, too, had envied Jennica's hair. At least two Wives and one Husband visited Tawny.

"But, you know, Jennica is not as perfect as she seems," one whispered.

"What do you mean?" I asked, fascinated by this tidbit of gossip.

"You should see her in yoga class," she offered. "In shavasana—you know, corpse pose, at the end of class—her breasts point straight toward the ceiling."

"A boob job?" I whispered.

She nodded, raising her eyebrows, as she continued her stroll.

But a divorce or Husband's death could mean walking papers for a Wife of Colfax Meadows. When the former owner of my house suffered her third divorce, she fled to Idaho. Too many memories, too big a house, too large a mortgage, or loss of membership in the marriage club—I suspected all might account for the exodus of the widowed and divorced Wives.

To become a Wife of Colfax Meadows, I'd have to marry a man like a Husband of Colfax Meadows. So I began to study that species, too. Like Jennica, her husband checked all the boxes. A USC grad with Ken doll looks, Bruce had followed his father into finance. He leased such a mercurial parade of luxury cars—BMWs, Mercedes, and Jaguars—I could never look out my window and know for sure that Bruce was home. He smoked cigars on the deck overlooking his pool, perhaps celebrating an IPO, and chatted on his cell—with a colleague, friend, client, lover, who knew—swearing every third word. When we happened to cross paths, he perused my dusty Corolla with a hint of disdain. But I had to hand it to Bruce, his financier's poker face usually won out.

Another Husband walking his rottweiler stopped to talk one day as I exercised Rex and Shane. "You know, my dog dreamed about your dog last night," he said. I giggled at his charming pleasantry. But when he said the same thing the next week, I didn't smile. This line of conversation was going nowhere good.

Of course, there was that other Husband of Colfax Meadow—Robert Blake, now standing trial for his wife's homicide. I had that Husband to observe, too.

I suspected that I could never become a Wife of Colfax Meadows, any more than an aardvark could become an armadillo. A nip here, a tuck there, a highlight here, a blind eye there wouldn't cut it. Besides, maybe I didn't *want* to be a Wife of Colfax Meadows. True, I envied their built-in companionship, their automatic status as wives and mothers, their shared purpose raising children alongside their Husbands. But another part of me did not envy them at all. In my singledom, I could devote hours to pursuing all manner of odd fancy—as I had when studying to become a certified graphologist, enrolling in psychic college, or accepting an intriguing but low-paying job as a writer at a convent. And, on vacation, I could explore wherever, be it the Reclining Buddha in Bangkok or a candlelit celebration of Day of the Dead in Patzcuaro.

Still, I was haunted by my status as an outsider in Colfax Meadows. The neighborhood felt like a wide-screen, technicolor movie that I could relish, but only as a member of the audience, never as part of the cast.

Perhaps it was time to heed my professor's advice from long ago: "Stop trying to fit in. You'll never be normal."

Chapter 39

HUGGING SAINT

"But how the heck do I capitalize on my differentness?" I asked Neville over drinks at El Coyote, my favorite Mexican restaurant.

"First, let's define 'differentness,'" Neville said in his usual calm, seer-like voice. "Because I think you view that word as a negative, like, you know, the odd man out."

"You're right. My attitude is, 'The hell with my differentness. Why can't I just fit in and become a Wife of Colfax Meadows?'"

"Look at it this way," Neville said. "The things that make you different and set you apart from others are your very gifts. They are what you bring to the world. So don't cry over your differences, revel in them."

"So, what *are* my differences?"

"That sounds like a question for a career counselor."

"Or maybe God."

"Or the next best thing: a saint. In the *Whole Life Times* this week, I read that the Hugging Saint is coming to town. Let me grab the article from my car. Maybe she can answer your question."

A few minutes later, as I sipped a margarita, I skimmed the story. Amma, or "mother," was a powerful Indian guru who had hugged more than ten million people "to spread selfless love and compassion toward all beings." During her upcoming North American tour, she planned to stop in LA, where she would conduct a fifteen-hour hugging session. Followers said she performed miracles. She diverted storms. She turned water into pudding. But the miracle that most interested me was her purported ability "to erase all worries and transmit unconditional love with a single hug."

Ever since I'd broken up with Mel, I'd harbored a crimp in my heart. Yes, living with Peter had helped. So had prayer, meditation, and journaling. But none of these balms totally quelled the niggling pain. If my heart was bigger, I surmised, I would have loved Mel in spite of his issues. Turning down his marriage proposal had called into question my capacity to love. Worse still, maybe Mel had been my last chance at marriage, and I'd thrown it all away.

I knew I needed help defining my calling. But maybe, right now, what I needed more was the unconditional love of a saint.

When I arrived at the Westin Hotel in Van Nuys, an attendant gave me a token with a number on it. "R-37" didn't sound promising. And it wasn't. A disciple, dressed in a loose white tunic and pants, told me it meant a six-hour wait, well past midnight. As a reserved Midwesterner, I had resisted the Southern California custom of greeting almost everyone with a hug. I smiled at the irony of waiting hours in a fluorescently lit ballroom for the chance to hug a stranger.

At 2 a.m., the "Rs" were instructed to get in line. We had to remove our shoes and store our belongings in a bin before we inched on our knees closer to Amma, who sat perched on a red velvet throne on a stage. I asked the attendant how Amma could maintain this pace, hugging people all night long without a break, meal, or even a trip to the restroom.

"She is connected to the eternal energy source," the attendant said with a half-smile. "She's not a battery that gets used up."

One by one, people dropped at Amma's feet and let her cradle them. In a span of five minutes, she dried the tears of a crying baby, assigned a mantra to a security guard, and blessed a couple about to marry.

All of a sudden, I was next. Amma pressed my face to her bosom and whispered in my ear—something that sounded like *mamamamama* in her native Hindi. Her grip was surprisingly firm considering I was probably her thousandth hug of the night. After about eight seconds, with a final squeeze, she released me and pressed a Hershey kiss and rose petal in my palm. An attendant steadied me as I hopped off the stage.

I stumbled to a chair nearby. I was lightheaded and elated, similar to how I had felt when I ventured into certain pockets of the convent, where only the nuns worked. Now I had piggybacked off Amma's divine connection just as I had with the monastics at the convent.

Collecting myself, I wandered into the lobby where booths sold incense, Kriya beads, jewelry, and Amma's books. As I perused the merchandise in a daze, I overheard two women chatting. "My reading with Xavier was a miracle," one observed. "Who knew Vedic astrology could be so helpful?"

"Excuse me," I said, my curiosity overcoming my usual shyness. "I hope I'm not intruding. But do you mind if I ask about your reading?"

"Not at all," the women chimed in unison. "Xavier is Amma's official Vedic astrologer. He travels with her on tours, giving readings thirty or sixty minutes long. Let me give you his card."

I climbed into bed, exhausted. As I lay there, I realized the tiny grip in my heart was gone. I grabbed my diary to commemorate the momentous occasion.

> *A short hug dispelled my anxiety about my broken engagement to Mel. It's almost as if Amma inserted herself in my thoughts to tell me, "Your track record of broken romances does not define you as unloving or unlovable." Suddenly, I realize every second, every person, every animal, every situation, presents an opportunity to give and receive love. Romance is one venue, to be sure, but by no means the only one. This woman, born in a low caste in southern India, has, indeed, performed a miracle. And far more significant than turning water into pudding! She's taught me, without saying a word, that I am a loving person.*

Chapter 40

XAVIER

The next morning, I logged onto Xavier's website and read his childhood bio. From a young age, he'd been fascinated with the cosmos. In an old family snapshot, the teen sat cross-legged on his bedroom floor, in front of walls plastered with posters of the planets, constellations of stars, and the earth viewed from outer space. Eventually, he chose a more practical pursuit, rising to senior management in finance. But in 1990, when he met Amma on her North American tour, he abandoned his career, sold his house in Vancouver, and moved to Amma's ashram in southern India.

His Vedic astrology readings, according to his website, helped clients identify their strengths and weaknesses and "optimize their potential to live according to their true destiny." *Wow,* I thought, *sign me up!*

Finding my birth certificate buried in the garage had been propitious. I retrieved the yellowed parchment and noted my exact time of birth: December 19 at 6:22 p.m.—"after a Friday night fish dinner," my mother had noted. I booked my astrological reading for the following Saturday.

I knocked on the door of the designated house in West LA. I assumed it was owned by an Amma devotee. A woman with pink cheeks and an artfully wrapped white turban invited me inside. Immediately I could feel the vibe—a lot of meditation occurred in this home.

"Have a seat," she said, pointing to a puffy L-shaped couch. "Xavier will be with you in a moment."

I sat down and closed my eyes. The ebullient calm of the room dispelled the angst of my rush to make it on time. I took out a spiral notebook to jot down my questions: *Based on my astrological chart, what are my differences? How do they define my calling? And what should I do about guys?*

Just then, Xavier appeared. Tall, rail-thin, with large blue eyes, he wore an Indian tunic and a long strand of sandalwood beads that accentuated his height.

"Come on in," he said, showing me to a chair in a small office. No tarot deck, incense, votive candles, or other spiritual accessories graced the desk—just a razor-thin black laptop. Even ancient Vedic astrology had gone digital.

He brought the straightforward, humble demeanor that I'd observed in other Canadians. In a low, sonorous voice, he asked, "Any particular question you have, Miss Collister?"

"Well, basically about career and love," I replied. "The usual, I guess." I had already forgotten the questions I'd jotted down.

"Fine, let's begin with work."

I produced a tiny tape recorder from my purse. "Do you mind if I tape this?"

"Not at all. Good to have a recording to listen to again." He gave me a look as if to say, *Okay, are you ready to hear what the heavens have to say?*

I clicked on the recorder and nodded.

He slid his laptop over so I could see my astrological chart—a circle divided into quadrants, filled with icons and diagonal lines, set against a celestial blue background.

"What I notice most," Xavier began, "is that Mercury rules your chart. That is the planet of communication. So your work properly relates to words, be it the spoken or written."

I was impressed already.

"This would be a good chart for, say, someone who is a writer, teacher, counselor, therapist, social worker, some occupation where you're communicating with other people. But coupled with your role as a communicator is your Virgo soul. Being of service is what your soul needs. And that is the way to transcend your karma."

"So, communication in service to others?"

"Exactly."

"Okay, what about romance?"

Xavier hesitated, obviously carefully choosing his words. "Virgo is the place in the zodiac where Venus, the planet of love, is debilitated. It's at its weakest. So when people with a Virgo soul look for support from a partner, they have a hard time finding it."

"You've just described my last two decades of dating."

I could hire a soothsayer to remove a curse. But a debilitated Venus, embedded in my celestial DNA? That sounded impossible to rectify.

Xavier went on. "Relying on support outside yourself is a real trap for you. That's because the core issue in your chart is to become strong and self-reliant, to get past the idea that support somehow resides outside of you. You have to develop it internally."

I gulped. He was describing the very antithesis of my "white picket fence" dream.

"It's not that many people won't add a great deal to your life," Xavier added, to soften the blow. "It's just as a permanent solution, your work providing service to others will be the most rewarding. It won't disappoint you the way people sometimes will." He paused and then added, "Let's be clear. In Western culture, romantic love has replaced religion as the place people seek meaning, transcendence, joy, and wholeness. But that paradigm just doesn't work for you. You need to find your wholeness in service, not in coupledom."

He went on to say that my chart supported education for the next three years. "So if you want to go back to school to pick up a new skill, now is an ideal time."

I listened to Xavier's audiocassette in my car, as I wended my way home through the evening rush hour. What amazed me was how his observations dovetailed with so many others'. My long-ago career counselor, after multiple assessments, came to the same conclusion as my ruling planet Mercury. She, too, had recommended an occupation in communication.

And Xavier's assertion that I look within for support reminded me of my old dream—of walking down the church aisle only to discover at the altar that I was marrying myself. Now that dream made sense.

As far as the service component, the owner of the psychic college had once told me, "Eighty percent of your pleasure as a spirit comes from healing others. You have a skill in this area. You cut yourself off from your spiritual nature by not allowing yourself to do what gives you so much pleasure, that is, to heal people."

And I couldn't forget the definition of "witch" that I'd looked up in an occult dictionary while dating the likely male witch, Purple Person: "The craft of a witch is to alleviate the pain and suffering of fellow human beings, bringing them much-needed solace and succor."

Even the womanizer Brandon had alluded to my service inclination. In our final conversation, he had said, "One of the things I admire about you is your ability to nurture and heal." Maybe the mission statement I'd found in my garage—"heal with words"—had been spot-on. All those iterations of it had paid off.

And who knows, if I helped the suffering as my profession, maybe I wouldn't need to be doing it in my romances. No more "only basket cases need apply."

When I got home, I called Neville. "I can't thank you enough for showing me that article about the Hugging Saint." I told him about Amma's banishing all of my anxiety following my breakup with Mel and about Xavier's recommendation—communication, but with a service component.

"Yeah, writing three thousand 'Dear John' letters doesn't exactly carry a service component," he noted wryly. "But then I should talk. So much of what I write doesn't do jack shit for anyone either."

"I hear ya."

Neville, in a confession out of sync with his usual confidence, responded, "My deepest fear is that I'll die without having mattered."

"At the end of your days, you want to say, 'God, look at what I did with the talents you gave me.'"

"Yeah, to not be a 'worry and a weeping of unused wings.'"

"Exactly. Who wrote that?"

"A poet and painter named Kenneth Patchen. I think the exact quote is: 'Man is not a town where things live, but a worry and a weeping of unused wings.'"

We both fell silent. There was nothing left to say. I suspected that quote defined both our lives more than we cared to admit.

Chapter 41

EARTHLY REALM

Much as I trusted Xavier's guidance, I wanted a second opinion. I opted for the most credentialed career counselor I could find—the president of a career development association, who was also a professor of career development at Santa Monica College—a far cry from my very first career coach, young and fresh out of school.

I arrived early at Arianna's office, located on the second floor of the college. We chatted about the cybermarketing class I was taking in the school's business department. Then she stopped and said, "Well, I believe I know what you should be."

"So soon, even before I take any assessments?"

"Oh, after my years in this field, I can tell just by feel what someone should be."

"Alright," I said. She was so confident, I dismissed my doubts.

"I think you belong in counseling."

"Really?"

"Yes, I'm sure of it."

I marveled at how her choice matched Xavier's reading. Now I had confirmation from the earthly realm.

Arianna smiled. "I'd recommend the program where I earned my MS—Cal State Northridge. Let me give you the name and number of the department chair."

I returned to my car in a pink cloud. After a long period of wrongness, I felt this enormous sense of rightness.

Back home, I checked the MS program online. Since I hadn't majored in psychology as an undergrad, I'd have to complete twelve units of prerequisites in addition to a sixty-unit core curriculum. I'd also have to earn six hundred internship hours, as well as write a master's thesis. All in all, the program would take three years and cost tens of thousands of dollars.

My God, I thought, *can I hack that much school, endure a forty-five-minute commute from my house,* and *afford tuition on top of living expenses in one of the costliest cities in the US? And what about my classmates? Can I attend class with students half my age? Will they accept me? Will I accept them?*

I scrambled through my purse for the name and number of the department chair Arianna had given me. Maybe he could put my concerns to rest. I called his secretary and booked an appointment for the following week.

I knocked quietly at the professor's door.

"Come on in," he called out.

I opened the door to find a tiny office lined floor to ceiling with books. He was furiously typing at a computer with his back to me.

"Have a seat," he said without turning around.

I sat for a good five minutes without seeing his face. Feeling increasingly uncomfortable, I finally said, "Maybe this isn't a good time."

He whipped around. He was a tall Black man in his fifties with large, gold wire-rimmed glasses.

"Dr. McMannus," he said, extending his hand.

"Laurie, Laurie Collister," I said, trying to regain my composure. "Nice to meet you. Arianna, your former student, suggested I meet with you."

"Ah, Arianna, one of my top students. I'm trying to get her to teach here."

"She said I might be a good fit for your program."

"I trust her opinion."

I told him about my desire to transition into counseling after a twenty-year career in PR, journalism, and marketing communications. In spite of our rocky start, Dr. McMannus proved as enthusiastic as Arianna. "I believe you'd be a good fit here," he said. "Just submit your transcripts and application. If everything looks good, I'll grant you permission to earn your prerequisites once you're in the program. The next semester starts in late August."

After our meeting, I wandered around the campus in a daze. It was flat and treeless, and the buildings were large nondescript rectangles. The ninety-degree heat reflected off the cement concourse. I grabbed a bite in the cafeteria, soaking in the din of students chatting and the rock music playing on the sound system.

As I spooned mouthfuls of cherry yogurt, about all I could digest after my emotional morning, I thought about Xavier's words: "You have a three-year window that is excellent for education." I felt like God was tossing breadcrumbs, leading me out of my heart of darkness. All I had to do was follow the trail.

After I submitted my application and academic transcripts, my acceptance letter came with amazing dispatch. Dr. McMannus's signature—tall, full, with flourishes—was just as enthusiastic as his demeanor that hot day in his office.

I called Neville to tell him the good news. "After being lost for so long," I said, "I feel found."

He then told me about the meeting he'd had that afternoon with an IT guy who came to fix his computer. "Your hard drive is like a plane hangar," the guy pointed out. "And your applications and programs are using what amounts to a small closet in that vast space."

"How poetic."

"I think your life is like that closet, Laurie. Maybe your new direction will take advantage of all that capacity that has gone untapped for so long."

"You think so?"

"Definitely. Remember how your mother said you were a late bloomer?"

"Yeah, all too well."

"Well, maybe you're finally beginning to bloom. I know you've equated blooming with getting married and having children. But maybe, karmically, you were meant to work on lessons in this life that don't have anything to do with a man or progeny. Maybe the lessons have to do with the path you're about to take."

"I hope you're right."

"Oh, I think I am. And why wait? Why not start right away? Just add 'MS (in progress)' to the top of your resume. That way you can get a job in counseling to help pay for your tuition and begin building experience."

"But where?"

"You're always talking about 'home,' 'being at home,' 'finding a home.' The homeless could be the first population that you serve."

Chapter 42

MISSION

After I got off the phone with Neville, I entered "homeless" as a search term in an online job site. Hundreds of positions popped up. LA had not yet achieved its status as the homeless capital of America, but it was quickly moving in that direction. The next evening, I spotted an opening for an employment counselor at a hundred-year-old homeless shelter and men's recovery program on downtown LA's skid row.

I shut off the computer and took a long walk. I felt a flood of rightness that I wanted to luxuriate in before I crafted my cover letter. Only a handful of times had I experienced that same delicious sensation before taking some definitive action—like a move to a new city, a long overdue breakup, or a career change. My premonitions always came true; the decision turned out to be the right one. I knew this one—getting a job at a skid row mission—would turn out right, too. My calm and well-being only grew when I emailed my resume and cover letter to the mission's HR director.

When I woke up the next morning, I had gotten a reply already. The HR director invited me to interview "at my earliest convenience."

The next morning, I donned a skirt and blouse and headed to the most dangerous street in LA. I exited the freeway and made my way downtown past the county courthouse, past lawyers and secretaries hurrying to their jobs, then by Starbucks, a line of customers spilling out its door.

This won't be so bad, I thought. But as I drove west on San Pedro Street, the main drag of skid row, the atmosphere quickly changed. Minivans sped by with names stenciled across their sides—THE MIDNIGHT MISSION, SALVATION ARMY, and LOS ANGELES MISSION. A shirtless pedestrian, with his black shoulders gleaming in the sun, did a fast set of chin-ups on a corner lamppost. A fluorescent yellow bike wove in and out of traffic. A boom box, bungee-hooked to its rear, played Marvin Gaye's "Mercy Mercy Me."

A woman pushed a baby carriage filled with Chihuahuas, their tiny paws braced on the pram's guardrail. Her companion tugged on a tight skirt barely covering her bottom. For a brief second, she yanked her tube top down, exposing her wares to potential customers.

Pedestrians walked straight into oncoming traffic, oblivious to crosswalks and stoplights. I swung my wheel to dodge them, as if navigating the joystick of a high-stakes video game. At Fourth and San Pedro, a barefoot man climbed on the hood of my car.

"What the hell!" I shouted.

He pressed his face into my windshield, glaring at me through the glass like a Halloween ghoul. I locked my doors, clicked on my windshield wipers, and zigzagged.

He tightened his grip.

"Get off!" I yelled, pounding on the windshield. "Get off my car!"

Finally, he let out a little laugh. "Have a nice day, lady," he said, as he slid off my hood and sauntered away.

By the next stoplight, I was hyperventilating and sweating—in no state to make a good impression at my job interview. I locked my doors repeatedly to make sure they were really locked. In the distance, I spotted my destination. A structure that looked like a medieval castle loomed on the horizon.

I circled the block-long complex searching for the parking entrance. The slow revolution in rush-hour traffic gave me a chance to calm down and think. Maybe I should just keep driving. Blow off the interview. Flee this hellhole while I had a chance.

I wanted to follow my calling. But did I have to risk my life in the process? On the other hand, I had to be practical. I had absolutely no experience in the counseling profession. I would be lucky to get *any* job, even on a dire street like this one.

The parking entrance suddenly appeared. I slowed down and inched into the narrow opening. The nose of my car dipped down the ramp. I disappeared into the dark subterranean garage.

"Oh Lord," I whispered. "Here I go."

Chapter 43

CABAL

I rolled down my window at the guard gate. "I'm Laurie Collister, here to see Mr. Stockton."

The attendant scanned a list of names on a clipboard. "Yes, I see you here, Ms. Collister. Come this way." He led me to a spot in the corner of the garage.

As I got out of my car, a dark form shot by. I leapt back, dropping my resume portfolio.

"Oh, that's Storm," the attendant said, glancing up as he recorded my license plate on his clipboard. "Don't mind her."

"Your resident cat?" I asked, catching my breath. A well-fed black cat studied me with luminescent yellow eyes, its tail slowly waving.

"She keeps the rats at bay," he explained. "They were eating employees' cars before she came along."

"A rat can eat a *car*?"

"They like to gnaw on the engine wires, especially when they're warm and chewy," he explained. "The rats on skid row are on the big side." He held his hands a foot apart. "Let's just say, they get what they want."

I gathered my things and made my way to the elevator. As I waited, I watched my still-warm Toyota. I hoped Storm would do her job.

A man joined me at the unusually slow elevator. He was the best-dressed man I'd ever seen. A paisley silk handkerchief in his breast pocket matched his tie. His wheat-colored, pin-striped suit highlighted his golden-brown skin. When he shot me a smile, I asked, "Can you tell me where the front desk is? I'm here for a job interview."

"Sure, I'll lead you there. My name is Anthony, by the way," he said, sticking out his hand. "I'm head of Residential Services."

If the rats aren't friendly, at least the people are, I thought. He held the elevator door for me, and we ascended to the lobby.

The receptionist handed me a job application and pointed to one of the upholstered chairs lining the lobby. It had been a long time since I'd tackled this kind of form. Squeezing who I was into one page was not easy. I pondered the reference section. A nun at my previous full-time employer—the Hindu convent—might scare off the HR director. I settled on Neville. He'd know the right thing to say.

I glanced out the tall picture window behind me. Dozens of homeless men filled the courtyard, prone under army blankets or leaning against a pile of what I imagined were all their worldly possessions. One man stormed back and forth screaming over and over, "Who stole my shit?" Apparently, he'd left for a moment and returned to find his belongings missing. His distress heightened my own as I waited to be ushered into the mission's inner chambers.

"Are you finished, Ms. Collister?" the receptionist called from behind the counter. "Mr. Stockton will see you now."

The head of HR led me to a small, fluorescently lit, windowless office. He was a puffy man of a certain age—fifty-something—and obviously settled in his job. "Tell me, Ms. Collister, why do you want to work here?"

I wanted to tell the truth—"because I feel homeless"—but I decided that might not be the right answer. Instead, I responded with "It would be a privilege to join a hundred-year-old agency solving LA's most serious problem." I'd worked in PR for a decade. I knew how to lay it on thick.

He continued with another stock question: "How would a friend describe you?"

I wanted to say, "A professor once told me, I'm too different to fit in." But once again, I steered clear of the raw truth. "Deliberative. Far more of a listener than a talker."

Mr. Stockton nodded. He wasn't listening. He was operating on autopilot. "How would they describe your greatest weakness?"

"I consider all angles, so sometimes it takes me a while to make a decision."

He didn't point out that my weakness mirrored my strength. Instead, he checked his watch and abruptly stood up. "Senior management wants to meet you now." He led me up a floating staircase to the executive suite, then opened a door to a mahogany-paneled room overlooking the skyline of downtown LA. A group of all men, all in their fifties and sixties, all white except for one, lined a twenty-five-foot conference table. *Now the real interrogation begins*, I thought, *and by a cabal, no less.*

They looked assured of their place in the world as managers, fathers, husbands, and homeowners—the very opposite of the men they served. As they clutched their mugs of coffee, I noticed most wore identical gold signet rings, some on their pinky fingers, some on their right ring fingers. They all hailed from the same club, whatever that might be. Was this a job interview or a fraternity hazing?

My interrogators explained that the position I was applying for—as a career counselor / job developer—was the first of its kind in the mission's hundred-year history. "We have to be very selective about who we choose," the CEO began, watching me for a long moment. Was I that special person? He wasn't sure. "How would you develop a portfolio of employers who'd hire our guys?" he asked.

I took a deep breath. "Well, first, I would have to learn what your clients offer in terms of job skills. Then, working with a business reference librarian, I'd create a list of employers most interested in those skill sets."

The men nodded, seemingly pleased with that line of reasoning.

"But what about a guy who just got out of prison after twenty years?" the COO, a tall Black man, shot back from the end of the table. "What would you do for him?"

"Whether a man operates lawfully or unlawfully, he *still* develops skills."

The COO chuckled. "Yeah, I guess you're right on that score."

As the men sized me up, I had a chance to take in more of the room. Two dozen framed pictures filled every square inch of wall space. They were photos of more middle-aged white men, presumably the board of directors. I had to make the cut not just with the cabal before me, but also with this second, hidden cabal.

Back in Mr. Stockton's office, we started talking money. I told him I needed $10,000 more than the salary he offered.

"We'll have to go to the board on that," he huffed. "I doubt they'll agree."

That ended *that* discussion.

As I drove home, I had no idea what would happen. I longed for the challenge of skid row, and the chance to solve my own sense of homelessness as I helped others solve theirs. And, of course, the job fit in perfectly with my mission statement—"heal with words"—and at a mission, no less. At the same time, I felt anxious. My interview had pushed two hot buttons: rejection by a secret club—the cabal—and asking for what I needed only to be denied.

I knelt by my bed that night to say my prayers. "God," I whispered, "it's in your hands now."

Three days later, at 4 p.m. on a Friday afternoon, my cell phone rang. I didn't answer it or even look to see who'd called. Stretched out on a chaise lounge next to my parents' pool in San Diego, I'd left all worldly matters behind. The weekend had already started for me. Their dog, Poodle Bella, wedged her snout between my thighs as I ran my fingers through her top knot. My stepfather, Bill, slid open the patio door, ducked his head out, and asked, "Red or white?"

"Red, please."

"Gotcha."

I glanced at my watch. I just wanted to relax, not respond to anyone. But I couldn't help myself. I had to see who'd called. I tapped in my password and saw a ten-second voicemail from Mr. Stockton. I knew instantly why he'd called: I must have gotten the job. Employers rejected you by email or letter, never by phone.

I listened to his message: "Call me. It's urgent." I called him back immediately.

"I got you the extra $10K," he began. "I'd like to offer you the job if you're still interested."

"Thank you!" I said without hesitating.

We agreed on my start date in two weeks—April Fool's Day.

And so, just like that, my life took a dramatic left turn. I savored the news, just as I had when I first spotted the job listing. After applying, I'd shut off my computer, taken a long walk, and luxuriated in the premonition that I'd found my spot in the world, someplace I was meant to be. Now, I gazed at the hummingbirds as they dipped their beaks in a feeder of sugar water and ravens as they wove back and forth across the turquoise sky.

Bill handed me a heavy-pour glass of cabernet. As I sipped it, alongside Bella, Bill, and Mom, I kept the news to myself. I needed to get used to the idea—to wrap my head around the adventure that lay ahead—before I shared it with anyone. I was about to join a world where rats ate cars, where a pedestrian did a quick set of chin-ups on a lamppost, where people slept and died outside your window, and where I might be of use . . . or not.

Chapter 44

THE BEAT

On the afternoon before my first day of work, I decided to fortify myself. I needed all the sustenance I could muster. And where better than at the convent? No other place had imbued me with such peace. Of course, I could no longer wander through the offices of the monastics, breathing in their divine union. But the convent's tiny chapel, on the first floor of the fellowship's administration building, was open to the public for a few hours each afternoon.

I thought that once I'd resigned from my three-year position as a writer, the magic would be lost forever. Not so. As I stepped into the building's lobby, the quiet ecstasy came flooding back.

I nodded to the receptionist, a nun dressed in a navy blue sari, the uniform of a novitiate, then I gently pushed open the door to the chapel. The light was so dim I could barely make my way to a seat near the altar. As my eyes adjusted, I marveled that I was not alone. A good dozen devotees sat quietly in the gloom, their eyes closed, heads tilted slightly heavenward, hands placed palms up on their knees, in divine communion.

Sinking into meditation in the chapel came so much easier than being alone in my bedroom. The vibe—permeated with the founding guru's spirit and nearly a century of monastics' prayers and meditation—felt like a wave that I could catch and glide along. How ironic, I thought. I'm sitting in possibly the most peaceful spot in LA when the very next day I'll start work in the most chaotic one.

That evening, I laid out the outfit I'd wear for my first day at the mission. I'd long since retired my wardrobe of business suits—mandatory attire for career women in the 1980s. I selected black cigarette slacks, slim but not too tight; black suede ankle boots; and a gray blouse with an artful twist at the bodice.

On my dresser top, I made room for my jewelry—silver hoops and a long shiny chain with a pendant in the shape of a lotus—a symbol of awakening in the Hindu religion and a reminder of the pink lotuses floating on the convent pond. The outfit was far more my style than the bright blue suit with gold buttons and pleated skirt I had worn for my ill-fated job interview at the film studio.

And my bedroom felt more like me, too. After escrow closed on my house, the former owner had called to ask for the drawer pulls from her sons' dresser. Her little boys missed them. And so, one by one, I unscrewed the handles in the shape of pinwheels, baseballs, and airplanes, and replaced them with my choice—antique brass fixtures.

I no longer felt like I was squeezing into someone else's shoes. The room had slowly begun to fit my own contours. There was my altar featuring an eight-inch-tall Ganesh. My shelves of diaries and books. My purple yoga bolster to slip under my knees when I meditated. And my tall, four-poster brass bed with a brand-new pillow-top mattress.

I stretched out on my bedspread, not quite ready to climb under the covers. Even hours after leaving the convent, I could still feel its effects—the rightness and bliss. I thought about how I'd fare on skid row. I might last fourteen days or fourteen years. I didn't know. What mattered was that, for once, I was taking the first step to fulfill my vow: "heal with words." And, like all first steps, it was the hardest step of all.

I dialed Neville for a little moral support.

"Wish me luck," I said when he answered.

"Oh, right, tomorrow's the big day."

"It feels like a whole new chapter."

"Yeah, you're opening the door to the second half of your life."

"What do you mean?"

"Well, the first half of life is about making your way in the world—renting your first apartment, getting a job, buying a car, paying bills, finding a mate."

"Or not," I pointed out.

"True. Finding a mate or not. Raising children or not."

"And the second half of life?" As usual, I was enthralled by Neville's odd train of thought.

"The second half is really about looking within, following God's plan. The road map is no longer as clearly delineated. You have to develop your own road map, not the one your culture has dictated."

"That's what I've been doing these past few months."

"Yes, I've been watching you with great interest. Maybe I need to do the same. It's almost like what would either of us do if we understood that God was our employer?"

"Right. So at the end of our lives, we can honestly say, 'I used the talents You gave me in service to Thee.'"

"Exactly."

"But what about a man?" I asked him. "What about marriage? Where does all that factor in?"

"I think you're open to that. And that's good. It's always good to be open to connecting with whomever crosses your path, but . . ."

"But what?"

"But ultimately, you can't control whether you'll meet Mr. Right or not. You can't put your life on hold waiting for some mythical man who may or may not show up."

"True," I agreed quietly. I had learned that lesson the hard way.

"Besides, you have plenty of people in your life—your parents, your brother, me, your new colleagues at work, clients, God."

"So I won't be lonely living alone again?"

"No, you'll probably look forward to having time to yourself after nonstop interaction all day at work."

"Thanks, Neville, for your insight and your support. You know I don't take it lightly."

"I feel the same, Laurie. I think we're on the same soul train."

"On the fast train to . . ."

"Nowhere? No!" Neville laughed. "To somewhere! Now, get a good night's sleep. I'll be all ears about your first day. Call me!"

After I hung up, I knelt by my bed and lifted up the black dust ruffle. Neville had forgotten to mention Wally, who would keep me company, too. There, deep under my bed, he was fast asleep in his makeshift den. A friend had found the border collie galloping along Melrose in West Hollywood. He had posted LOST DOG signs and placed ads in the newspaper, but no one responded. And so, just like that, I had my first dog. With a yard, nearby doggie daycare, and Peter two doors down to pitch in, finally, I was in the position to properly care for my own dog.

Wally inched forward, gave me two wet kisses, then scooted back to resume his repose.

I slipped on my flannel pajamas and switched off the floor lamp. As I lay in bed, waiting for sleep to overtake me, I heard strange creaks and rustles. I still hadn't gotten used to the unfamiliar sounds of a new house. I rifled through my nightstand for earplugs. I warmed the wax between my palms and squeezed it in my ears.

The sounds stopped, but another remained. It was a faint beat deep in my ear canal. What was that? Slowly, it dawned on me. It was the beat of my own heart.

ACKNOWLEDGMENTS

First and foremost, a deep bow to my long-term writing teacher and mentor, Linda Schreyer. Without your good cheer and perceptive guidance, I never could have written this book.

A special thanks to my book coach, Candace Coakley. You were a wise and enthusiastic cheerleader. You took a fragmented set of chapters and showed me how to weave them into a publishable whole.

Much gratitude to She Writes Press, to CEO Brooke Warner and Project Manager Shannon Green. You led me through every step of the publishing process with unwavering warmth and professionalism.

Appreciation to Jill, my copy editor. What a miracle worker you are! You made each sentence, each paragraph, each chapter, so much better.

Kudos to my writing classmates—Darlene Basch, Paula Bernstein, Rick Draughon, and Sharon Dukett. Your perceptive critiques fine-tuned each chapter. I'm so grateful for your insight, companionship, and moral support.

Last, but not least, a huge thank-you to my family. To Peter Collister for agreeing to be included in such chapters as "Bachelor

Pad" and "Psychic College." To Jeri McGaw, for offering your encouragement and a tranquil setting in which to write. To Dan Collister for giving me your writer's mind. And, finally, to Bella, for lying next to me, be it the porch, office, or bedroom, always providing company and a cold nose in my ribs to tell me to take a break and go for a walk.

ABOUT THE AUTHOR

Laurie Collister is a counselor, journalist, and debut memoirist. After graduating from Kenyon College, she worked as a litigation paralegal, market analyst, investigative journalist, and, most recently, as a counselor on LA's skid row. In this checkerboard of professions, she learned how to harvest the hidden—key to penning *A Different Kind of Vow*. Her second memoir, about her fourteen years on skid row, will be published in 2027. Laurie lives with her extended family and dog Bella on a cul-de-sac in Los Angeles.

Looking for your next great read?

We can help!

Visit www.shewritespress.com/next-read
or scan the QR code below for a list
of our recommended titles.

She Writes Press is an award-winning
independent publishing company founded to
serve women writers everywhere.